Laurie Handlers is a Tantra Teacher, an intimacy coach and a Spiritual Leader. She holds a Master's in Education and a Bachelor's in Psychology and Sociology. Her career includes over thirty years as a corporate change consultant, individual empowerment coach and international seminar leader. She is a dynamic speaker, facilitator and has taught Butterfly Tantra courses since 1999. In addition she hosts an internet radio show *Tantra Café* on www.BBSRadio.com. Laurie is a global citizen and currently divides her time between the US, India and the UK.

October 6, 2023

SEX & HAPPINESS
The Tantric Laws of Intimacy

Joyce —

Laurie Handlers

I loved meeting you at the
Dames Conference. I hope
you enjoy this work of love,

Laurie Handlers

Butterfly Workshops Press
2702 E. Ironwood Drive
Phoenix, AZ 85028

Butterfly Workshops Press
2702 E. Ironwood Drive
Phoenix, AZ 85028

First Published, 2007

Second Edition, 2008

Third Edition, September 2019

© Laurie Handlers

© *Cover design:* Jeniffer Thompson at Monkey C Media
© *Front cover photograph:* Tom Kochel

ISBN-13: 978-0-9771740-0-3
ISBN-10: 09771740-0-X

Published by Laurie Handlers and printed by Ravi Sachdev at Allied Publishers Private Limited, 1/13-14 Asaf Ali Road, New Delhi–110 002, India

Dedication

To my parents,
Marty and Betty Handlers,
who taught me how to dance.

I would not know what the spirit of a philosopher might wish more to be than a good dancer.

— Friedrich Nietzsche

Important Caution
Please read this

The practices, disciplines and understandings in my book are not to be taken as specific medical, psychological, emotional, sexual or social advice, nor are they intended to be used as a diagnosis, prescription, or cure. Each person who may need a treatment program has individual needs and differences and should consult a licensed, qualified health care provider or other competent professional.

Acknowledgments

I especially want to thank Karin Cayford, my writing partner in this project. At first, she resisted the topic and then got so totally into it that sometimes I thought I was talking to myself. Without her incredible dedication, this book would not have gotten out of my mind and onto paper. And we had a lot of fun in the process.

I also want to thank Nan Temkin-Dudley, my college sister who agreed to read the manuscript, make initial edits and encouraged me to keep expanding it. Thanks to others who made edits along the way including Bill Plikaitis, Tom Bechtle, EllenSue Spicer-Jacobson, Rosemarie Mazur, and Amy Taylor. Finally, I must acknowledge Siobhan Mullally without whose editing, book design and overall publishing knowledge I might never have gotten the book done.

Huge thanks go to Gloria O'Neal who introduced me to Tantra in the first place. I know you had no idea the heights I would take Butterfly Tantra to in my career. Neither did I! You've made a big difference in the lives of so many people just by pointing me in this direction.

In addition, I want to thank Gloria Horrworth-Weisbrodt for being my professor and mentor, and for believing in me from the time we first met at The George Washington University many years ago.

Thanks to all my students. You inspired me to create the *Tantric Laws of Intimacy*. You tested the laws, reported back and together with you, this has been a work of love.

– L. H.

Dear Reader,

This book teaches you to observe your ways of thinking and behaving in relationship to intimacy. This is one of the biggest areas of pain in people's lives. What starts out so beautiful often ends up so truly painful.

My goal in writing this book has been to help myself and you by introducing you to ways of dealing and behaving differently from the you of before. It's a consciousness raising, if you will. Hopefully you will know to choose in the present moment rather than acting on the basis of programming from the past. It's about the power to respond from your "higher" self rather than being controlled by reptile brain which is fear-based.

The essence of transformation though is not just about you. It's about the whole world. As each person stops suffering, the world gets a little lighter. The world shifts from fear to love and from hatred to honor and from loneliness to intimacy.

If we lighten up, the world gets lighter – that is, there is more light in the world. Rather than worry how to go out and make a difference in the world, know that just by being more true to your "higher" self, you are making that difference in the world. It is that simple.

As you come to know for yourself how this book has helped you, I ask that you share the information with others for their empowerment as well. Please commit to telling the important people in your life about this book and this work. Tell as many people as possible. Tell at least fifty to a hundred of your friends and family. Consider buying them a copy and having them do the seminar with you. This is the meaning of life changing. And the bottom line is that it can become world changing.

That is really why I have written this book. It is to shift things on earth one book at a time. The more books out there, the more people in the courses will be getting happy on their very own. The more happiness in the world, the more love, the less suffering there will be. What a concept! Please do your part by spreading the word about this book and making sure that the people in your life have a copy. I know for me, it will make my biggest dream come true – women and men dancing in eternal ecstasy on earth now!

Thank you.
Laurie

Contents

Contents

Introduction

Women need a reason to have sex. Men just need a place.

– Billy Crystal

I heard a saying twenty-five years ago when I took my first step on the spiritual path: "We teach best what we need to learn." This is so true. To be honest I have only been one step ahead of my students in anything I've ever taught, one tiny step ahead since 1978, when I began leading workshops for women. I have used my life as a laboratory, teaching immediately all the lessons I ever got as soon as I got them. I admit the lessons haven't been so easy. I've distilled the principles that have worked for me and the insights I have gained into this book. They represent a lifetime of throwing myself into the fire, risking it all to see what might happen. Fortunately, you can read the *Tantric Laws of Intimacy* I developed without risking it all. I hope they work as well for you as they have for me.

The material offered here will sound as if I am talking right to you. As if you are in one of my courses. I meant it to be that way because I want you to get a true sense of who I am and what it is like to take Tantra courses with me.

The notion of the *Tantric Laws of Intimacy* came about during a conversation about what women want and what men want, and how despite the reams of material on relationships, they do not know about each other's wants, needs and desires. The first five laws just fell into my mental lap, as crisp and clear as the rules for chess or tennis. When I spoke in my courses about them, the next five laws surfaced just as easily, forming this book, *Sex and Happiness: The Tantric Laws of Intimacy.*

When I play tennis in a foreign country, I know exactly what to do because the laws of tennis are so well defined that they're understood no matter where you play the game. Games like tennis have rules, rules that we carefully teach our children and each other, rules that are understood and respected even when opponents don't speak the same language. There's no equivalent in the relationship game.

There are no clear and widely accepted laws of love, no established rules written into convenient manuals that are given to you on the eve of your graduation into sexual relations. This is why it's so difficult for people to have a great time being intimate. Attraction and sexual energy come knocking but they don't necessarily stick around. Happiness visits for fleeting moments, but it, too, fades in and out of our lives. We don't know how to keep love alive. We never learned the rules of love because no one else knew them. Some claimed to know them, but they are really teaching the wrong thing.

The sad truth is, there are no hard and fast rules we can all agree upon. We're pretty much on our own playing in the field of love, making it up as we go along with no coach, no team, and no instant replay. Thus we rarely get to make corrections to our intimate behavior, and so no connections. It seems that we just keep stabbing in the dark and end up wounding ourselves and others in the process.

For years I explored a multitude of roads leading to personal growth and awareness. These roads varied from well-traveled, popular thoroughfares to hacked-out trails in the wilderness. They were all valuable in their way. However, in 1996 I began studying Tantra with its emphasis on using the powerful energy that wells up naturally from the body's life and sex forces. Tantra provided the missing piece that enabled me to incorporate knowledge from those many different roads into a workable – and pleasurable – map for life. Tantra has affected my life so profoundly and so much for the better, that I'm determined to share it with everyone. There is of course, much more to it than exotic sexual practices. I am talking about the whole of my life, of having things I hardly dared dream of manifest in my life. Dreams can manifest in your life too.

Sex and Happiness: The Tantric Laws of Intimacy is really a self-portrait in words containing the knowledge I've garnered from a life of attempting to create fulfillment in relationships crammed with opposites: excitement-disappointment, joy-despair, happiness-resignation, poverty-abundance, and everything in between.

The way I teach transformation is to use whatever actually works for me in shifting my own life. I immersed myself in Tantra and it worked wonders, well beyond whatever I imagined. It altered my whole way of being as well as my career and my understanding of the world. So in developing my spin on modern-day Tantra, I have augmented the ancient practices with other disciplines that have also worked for me.

For example, I added emotional release techniques that I first experienced in women's consciousness raising groups and then in Bioenergetic courses I took in the '70's and even some Psychodrama practices I learned back then. I have added group process skills I learned at Carl Rogers' La Jolla Program and Neuro Linguistic Programming (NLP) practices such as "anchoring" and "reframing" as well. Often I employ trance states that I first learned from Milton Erickson, the famous NLP theorist.

What I believe sets me apart from other Tantra teachers is not just that I am writing from my own personal experience and in depth study, but that I am offering a roadmap to "creating possibilities" while working with people's intentions. This comes from my years at Landmark Education and my own corporate consulting business. I am committed to each and every person leaving my courses with something they truly came to receive.

Many teachers and writers helped me along the way, from Isabel Hickey to Osho, from Baba Ram Dass to Werner Erhart. I also learned from Carl Rogers, Alexander Lowen, Fritz Perls, Hanna Weiner, Moshe Feldenkrais, Jim Polidora, Robert Gass, Bodhi Avinasha, Barry Long, Daniel Odier, Joshua Smith, Greg Ehmka, Deva & Lakshmi, David Deida and Mohan. Direct visitations from Babaji now and then have added to my sense of confidence about what works even beyond what my rational mind believes. I've learned directly and indirectly from each of them about how to blossom in this life and I then developed the Tantric Laws of Intimacy you'll find in this book. They work. No doubt about it.

My book isn't exactly your typical Tantra book. It's based on Tantra because I found my own fulfillment through Tantra and I'll discuss Tantric principles and practices throughout the writing. It's a book about happiness, communication, self-expression, and sex - it's an intimacy book. The vision I "live into" on a daily basis is "Women and Men Dancing in Eternal Ecstasy on Earth Now!" This is my picture of intimacy.

As I read and re-read each lesson I say to myself, "Yes, that's true!" almost as if I'm seeing it for the first time. I'm learning the lessons over again every day. It's never-ending. Just when I sort out one huge thing and decide to kick back and eat bonbons, some other situation rises up and bites me on the ankle! We really do teach best what we need to learn. In my practice of Tantra, and even more through teaching it, I have learned to trust the process itself over my thoughts about the process, and have slowly come into a deep place of allowing inner and outer peace. I can certainly say I never expected to be here in this amazing place of bliss. Possibly you do not expect to be either. Hopefully, this book will make a difference to you in finding the way to your own place of peace being able to dance in ecstasy for yourself, with or without a partner.

Namaste (I bow to the divine in you)

Law X
Make Love in the Unknown

*The beauty of facing life unprepared is tremendous. Then
life has a newness, a youth; then life has a flow and freshness.
Then life has so many surprises. And when life has so many
surprises boredom never settles in you.*

– Osho

Let's start with sex. I was going to put this chapter at the end of
the book but then I thought about a special dinner my participants
engage in during one of my courses. At this dinner, dessert comes
first. It's always decadent deep chocolate and we feed it to each other
lingeringly to set the tone for dinner. Somehow, it just seemed right to
me to take the last law, the one about sex, and serve it as dessert first.

Sex Energy Is Life Energy

Sex energy runs the world. Whether you love sex or hate it; whether
you avoid, fear, worship or can't get any sex doesn't change that
situation. Sex energy makes the world go around, and coming to peace
with that notion and where you fit into the picture is what Tantra is all
about. Whenever Tantra says "sex energy," that means the life energy
itself – they're synonymous terms. When you see flowers blooming or
birds singing, the phenomenon is sexual. The flowers are blooming in
order to pollinate and reproduce. The birds are singing to attract a mate
and reproduce. It's a sexual dynamic.

Tantra is the ancient study of tapping into that sexual dynamic. It
includes practices designed to allow intense energy to circulate through
the body. In Tantra, you learn to tune into this energy, sometimes
solo, sometimes while in deep, open contact with another person. But
whether or not you have a partner, practicing Tantra will give you
more vitality and aliveness. It will bring your inner polarities into
balance, and allow you to be less frightened by the depths of your
own feelings.

The balance comes because there is an integration or unity principle
in Tantra, instead of a polarization or a duality. Tantra in Sanskrit means

"to weave". Tantra encompasses sensuality *and* spirituality. It encompasses darkness and light, wrong and right, and brings it all into the center of our awareness. Rather than seeing two sides as separate and distinct opposites, you see the unifying principle, the oneness of it all. In Tantra, Heaven is experienced on earth, in the body. It's not necessary to die in order to go to Heaven or to an afterlife filled with pleasure. You can experience the infinite in this life, in this body. Tantra is a spiritual practice of acceptance of all that is. It provides you the ability to have it all by weaving everything together and embracing it all.

Tantric exercises include both physical and mental meditation. Tantra can be said to be a somewhat accelerated path to higher consciousness because of the depth of the exercises which tap into the powerful sexual energy I was just speaking about. In Tantra, you are able to transform your behaviors, attitudes and even your appearance quickly and effortlessly through these meditations. In Tantra you achieve enlightenment by uniting the warring parts of yourself, which allows your divergent aspects to fall into natural balance. You learn to simply be present and open to what is, rather than sitting in constant judgment upon yourself or others, or wishing or trying to manipulate things into being other than what they ARE. No expectations, no checklist of things that will or won't make you happy, just being happy. It's very freeing for all aspects of your life including, but not exclusively, sex.

Sexual practices are the most written about but only one amongst the many forms of awareness practices in Tantra. Specifically, the sex act is not experienced as a relationship between subject and object, but rather as a communication between two aspects of self (masculine and feminine) or between two equal and open beings becoming one with each other and the universe. *Yab yum*, which is the Tantric symbol of union, is a union of god and goddess, Father Sky, Mother Earth, and all that exists in its ever-changing swirl of pure consciousness. In this union, there is no "self" and "other", but a true union of body, mind and spirit.

The Big O!

In a Tantra book with a chapter titled, *Make Love in the Unknown*, I imagine you're wondering about orgasms. Most Tantra books cover this subject. As a matter of fact, most western Tantra courses focus mainly on the sexual practices having to do with extended or one-hour orgasms.

Tantra is much more than that. But the sexual can open the way to the expansiveness of the spiritual. I prefer to have all of daily life about orgasm and bliss. I like the idea of having an orgasmic life! Orgasm is an expression of aliveness, of openness, of contact with others and life itself. But it is non-egoistic in Tantra. It is almost as if the "I" disappears and becomes nothing, it just IS, with no effort, at which point all becomes present and possible.

This state where there is only IS, where everything is present and possible is called *Mahamudra* in Sanskrit. Literally translated, *Mahamudra* means "great seal", and rests on emptiness, the absence of any meaning other than what your mind places upon it. Orgasm is an energy response of the whole being. It is not good, bad, fun, 'dirty', it just is. The "great seal" referred to is like that on correspondence in times past, when they would use sealing wax instead of glue to close an envelope, or instead of a lock and key to keep secure the box of important and most private documents the messenger was carrying.

These most secret, powerful practices were protected from prying eyes for many years as sacred esoteric teachings. Through Tantra, the power of sexual energy is able to render transformation, but only for the student willing to crack open their tightly sealed life and sense of self. To be open to emptiness, of letting go of the self-conscious and limited "I" to experience his or her infinite capacity for love, happiness, and bliss, not only for a selfish goal, but to share with others is what transformation is all about. In particular the Tantric lover can share this sublime ecstasy of orgasmic daily life with his or her beloved.

For my students and myself, the broadening of sexual pleasure is directly related to getting to know the mechanics of the body better; learning to express feelings, especially anger; tuning into and respecting pleasure preferences, their own at first, then their partner's; and directly communicating those wants and desires.

All these things are helped along by two essential Tantric practices: 1) proper breathing, and 2) maintaining *the witness*. By practicing these two things on a regular basis it's possible to let go of any feeling that cut us off from orgasmic pleasure. Really, that's what the rest of this book is about.

Beginner's Sex

Have you heard the Zen expression, *beginner's mind*? It's a way of viewing the world like everything in it is new. There is no expectation, no pain from a history of hurts and humiliations. Everything is experienced from an alert yet unguarded place. It's a fresh, open, childlike state of mind. Practicing Tantra is a path to this clear, childlike place, but it doesn't just happen. It takes work and training in meditation to come back to the open and loving place that is our natural state. That's because there's so much grief and rage to be dealt with between now and then, present and past, so much shame and guilt, and so many ideas in our own minds, and from society and past relationships, about how we *should* be in love, in relationship, and in sex. The beauty of Tantra is that it gets rid of all notions of 'should' and just permits us to feel, to be.

If I could distill all my advice about Tantra and sex into one sentence, that sentence would be, "Make love in the unknown." In answer to all your fears and doubts about sex, I'd simply say to you, "Bring back your beginner's mind. Come to the bedroom with no expectations. Come with openness in your heart for whatever happens."

But you would probably say in return, "Yeah, well, if I could do that I wouldn't need to read this book, would I?"

And you would be right. The purpose of practicing these *Tantric Laws of Intimacy* is to help you regain the natural, unguarded openness of your heart so that you can bring it to the most stressful and yet most rewarding area of your life – the bedroom. This takes some training.

Sex – Tantra Style

I remember once putting on fabulous drum music and sitting in *yab yum* with my partner. Yab yum is the powerful Tantric love-making position in which the man sits cross-legged, or with his legs straight out in front of him, and the woman sits directly in his lap with her legs wrapped around him. They look into each other's eyes and use conscious breathing techniques until all separation – time, space, and even gravity – fall away.

Yab Yum Position

As time passed and the music continued, my partner and I breathed together and gazed into each other's eyes. Our bodies began to undulate. We were drawn into higher and higher states of bliss and ecstasy. All time and space seemed to go away. When we finally stopped, we were amazed to find that three hours had passed. It was the most intimate space we had experienced, and yet my lover and I were both completely clothed.

Edward* talks about sitting in yab yum as a somewhat skeptical novice in one of my courses. The woman sitting in yab yum with him was also new to Tantra. They sat as instructed and gazed into one another's eyes, doing the prescribed breathing together. Then a strange and powerful thing happened. Without prior experience, they felt at the same time an almost electrical connection form suddenly between them at the level of the solar plexus, the third *chakra*, or energy center of the body as explained in traditional Eastern medicine. (This connection is often depicted in ancient Tantric illustrations as a golden light shining from the abdomen of one partner to the abdomen of the other.) Time fell away. Other students in the class ceased to exist for them. There was only this primal energy and connection and a sense of having tapped into something much larger than themselves.

* Some names have been changed, others have not. All quotes in the book are authentic.

Another time I remember that my lover and I put on blindfolds and started out from remote corners of a room, following only breath and inner guidance, moving only when authentic movement happened, until we found each other. (This is a version of an exercise I will discuss more fully later called *Latihan.*) It probably took a full hour to finally come together in the large and unfamiliar room. By the time we made contact, we were hungry for each other and fed upon the other in a feast of the senses.

Recently, I had an experience with a lover where we played for hours. We made an agreement that we would have no oral or penetration sex. As a matter of fact we kept on some of our clothing. We put on music with a hot Latin beat and began by gazing into each other's eyes for what seemed a very long time.

Then we started touching and moving to the music. We rubbed against each other; we nibbled on and then rubbed sensual fabrics over various body parts. We took it slowly; we weren't going for the release. As each level of pleasure would happen to us, we would make sure to look into the other's eyes. At some point we realized we were melting into the other over and over again. Sometimes we'd come back to our individual selves and say something, or giggle, but mostly we had a deep and vast experience of falling and melting.

Breathe and Make Love

Many people who hear of Tantra think it's just a series of sexual techniques. They call me up wanting to know about the *Kama Sutra*, delayed ejaculation, or "G" spot stimulation. In fact, many of the world's well-known Tantra teachers spend hour upon hour teaching their students "sacred spot" massage.

I, too, have a section of my beginner's Tantra course where we cover this subject in conversation. Yes, and I assign homework to both men and women to find and learn to stimulate the G spot for a different kind of sexual stimulation, one that doesn't have to peak into orgasm and then drop.

I also teach techniques and assign people homework to expand their capacity for pleasure, as in postponing ejaculation for men, and moving to many orgasmic peaks for women. (A more complete list of suggestions, one for men and one for women, appears on the following page.) Personally, however, I've gotten away from teaching people that precise, exact techniques will lead to enhanced love-making.

Barry Long, the famous Tantra teacher from Australia, once said, "In order to make love, you've got to make love." He didn't say, "In order to make love, you've got to find the perfect person, feel perfectly happy with that person, make sure that person is perfectly suited to your physiological needs in the bedroom, learn every sexual technique known to man, and then make love."

No. In order to make love, you've got to make love. But, of course, therein lies the rub; while love does make the world go around, almost everything in the world gets in the way of expressing love. This book gives you a ten-step program toward making peace with your demons so that you can actually make love with your lover. You will learn that in the spirit of this quest, sexual technique is helpful, but it's secondary to knowing yourself first to allow the deepest intimacy to be attained.

The following are two lists for expanding orgasm in women, and in men.

Techniques for expanding orgasm in women:

Breathing relaxation exercises

Tantric breathing and squeezing techniques

Self-exploration of the body

Masturbation, prolonging orgasm and continuing past orgasm

Vaginal push-ups and push-outs

G spot stimulation by yourself

Knowledge of your own body

Yoga

Full body massage to soft sensuous music

G spot stimulation by a partner

Knowledge of your partner's body

Clearly communicating sexual tastes and what you want

Being honest and open in all personal communications

Willingness to learn about your partner's body and desires

Being direct when angry

Anal stimulation

Being willing to be ravished and satisfied beyond the imagination

Being willing to do the same for your partner

Being treated and adored as a Tantric Goddess

Techniques for expanding orgasm in men:

Breathing relaxation exercises

Tantric breathing and squeezing techniques

Self-exploration of the body

Masturbation to the point of ejaculation, but without ejaculation, for 21 days to start, and then three times per week after that

Masturbation, prolonging orgasm and continuing past orgasm, without ejaculation

Rhythmical contraction of the genital area muscles, fifty times per day

Exercise that improves stamina, strength, and flexibility, such as Yoga

Squeezing each testicle once for every year of life, once per day

Knowledge of your own and your partner's body

Full sensual body massage

Being direct when angry

Clearly communicating your sexual tastes and what you want

Anal stimulation

Being willing to be ravished and satisfied beyond the imagination

Being willing to do the same for your partner

Being treated and adored as a Tantric God

A Few Points About These Lists

I will explain most of these practices in more detail on the pages shown, but to avoid them all seeming too much like a program that needs to be followed to the letter, I will discuss them in an organic, rather than systematic way. I have arranged the lists so you can begin solo, and then, as you develop more confidence and sexual fitness through these practices, you will feel ready to explore Tantra further with a partner.

A Basic Word About the Breath

I always recommend that people learn basic *breathing* and then *breathing and squeezing* techniques in order to train their bodies to open to pleasure and empty out pain. Later on, I'll show you how to do some of these breathing exercises.

Are they really necessary? You bet. Here in the West, we're taught that breathing is something you do when you're alive and stop doing when you're dead, and that's about the extent of it. As far as I'm concerned, though, even if you aren't intending to learn any Tantra, proper breathing is essential. Proper breathing alone will change your life due to the mind/body connection and the benefits proper breathing brings. Breathing and squeezing, contracting particular muscles in a very focused way is particular to Tantra, and helps channel the vital sexual energy which we are trying to tap into in order to achieve the higher levels of bliss and consciousness. The great thing is, anyone can breathe and squeeze, anywhere. How much more exciting when you finally get to do it with a partner to add to the pleasure for you both.

Pushing Your Own Boundaries

In addition to noticing your breath, it's also a good idea to explore boundaries and pleasure when you begin to study Tantra; to let go of any notions of 'right' and 'wrong' and allow yourself to be. I don't know how comfortable you are with masturbating, but one of my goals is to get you very comfortable with it, comfortable enough to experiment, to have fun, to learn about yourself.

If you practice some of the techniques from the lists on the previous pages for a minimum of 21 days, you can significantly expand your threshold for pleasure. In my world, more pleasure equals more love flowing – in all its forms – and that has to be good!

Go Play with Yourself

In my workshops I tell people that the Tantric practices will feel mechanical at first, like learning anything new – riding a bicycle, mastering a tennis serve, or learning a new dance. For this reason, even if you have a partner, it's important to practice the new skills only with yourself. If you practice too early with someone else, it might mechanize sex rather than enhance it. That might cause you to lose your excitement and get discouraged, and we definitely don't want that.

Your partner can also be studying at the same time, in a different room. This is not selfish; we all need to give ourselves permission to feel pleasure, and by doing it solo, there is no 'performance anxiety' or demands, both voiced and unsaid, which are expected to be met. There is nothing but relaxation, flow, peace. How much more bliss will you and a lover be able to share if your love making is based on that blissful frame of mind, rather than one of pressure and stress and desperate need for orgasm?

Once you get the sex-energy techniques into your own body so that they're no longer just mechanical actions, but practices that really work to enhance pleasure, you can share these techniques with your partner/s to enhance each other's satisfaction. It usually takes twenty one days to get them out of your head and into the body. NLP exerts say this is how long it takes to form a new habit. Once the practice of ejaculation control is in a man's body, it can just show up during sex or not. It will be in the flow of the dance appropriate to the specific session. Then the practice of Tantra can take you to a different consciousness altogether, a place where there is time/no time, space/no space, gravity/no gravity. In this place, whatever your religious background, you can experience unity with the One.

Practicing Tantra gives you access to *self-generated energy* that is internally accessible and at your command whenever you want it. I realize this goes against everything you've been taught about the nature of your own energy and the source of pleasure and excitement. The notion that you turn yourself on, that you all turn yourselves on, frees you from needing someone to come along from the outside and physically manipulate your body in just the right way to get your fires burning. Turning yourself on makes you non-dependent on an outside person for what and how much pleasure you feel. This doesn't lessen love or sexual connection; rather, it frees and expands it through self-nurturing.

Shanna writes: I had always known I had the capacity to be multiorgasmic, but becoming engaged to a man with a bad back, and then later married to an unmotivated partner with a low sex drive, made me think there was something 'wrong' with me for being interested in sex.

Thanks to masturbation, in particular G spot massage, I now know there is something incredibly 'right' about me. The first time I had a G spot orgasm, I could feel it tingling from my head to my toes. My mind was still and quiet, my whole body was flowing, wafting as light as air. The waves of orgasm were effortless, exciting, and yet totally calming at the same time. My inner voices worrying about whether or not I would come, and whether or not I was being selfish pleasuring myself in that way, were all silenced in the complete union of mind, body and spirit. It took a while, perhaps an hour, but there was no hurry, no one rushing me, no need to 'perform' or worry about anyone else for a change.

Once I got past the fear that I wouldn't orgasm, the undulations of pleasure rippled through me, and kept on going. It was far different from a clitoral orgasm. Like the difference between a volcanic eruption, earthquake and tsunami all in one, and a truck rumbling past my house.

I had considered myself fairly educated about sexuality and being a woman. Yet once I discovered this hidden treasure deep within myself, it was as though I was coming into my own body for the first time. It was a power unlike anything I had ever imagined, and it was all mine to do with as I chose. What a revelation. What bliss. With practice and training, I can orgasm easily now many, many times, solo whenever I choose, or with my partner. Some of our Tantric love making sessions go on for an hour or more, becoming either a series of several dozen shorter orgasms, or one continuous long orgasm. The beauty is, I can choose. And my partner finds them both equally exciting, in different ways, and is able to respond in a similar way, with no rest in between (refractory period), and orgasms that go on for minutes, not mere seconds.

My solo explorations empowered me to give myself the gift of my own pleasure. Once I was skilled at it, I was then able to share this gift with a lover who appreciates sharing my sexual energy and bliss, and does not feel the performance anxiety of having to 'give me' an orgasm.

Best of all, the sharing of this sexual energy is truly the 'gift that keeps on giving', for far from being depleted after us both having multiple orgasms, we can put in a full day's work in very demanding, stressful careers, and keep our cool and still have energy to burn.

Breathe and Make Noise

Years ago, when I read Betty Dodson's first book, *Liberating Masturbation* (renamed *Sex for One*), I realized that I was preventing myself from having orgasm at exactly the moment of orgasm by holding my breath. I would have the thought, "Oh, I think I'm gonna come!" Of course, by holding my breath and going into my head instead of staying in my body, I would actually not come. I was blocking orgasm, but I didn't know it until I read her book.

I took her advice and began to slowly teach myself to breathe throughout the sexual experience while I self-pleasured. How I would know I was breathing is that I would make sounds. If I was making noise, it was cool. If not, I was thinking and being in my head and often, without being aware of it, holding my breath.

Reading that book is how, years before I discovered Tantra, I realized that making noise was one of my secrets to pleasure. Now I know that noise-making involves so much more than just the voice box. In Tantra, we make **lots** of sounds. Making sounds helps you breathe instead of holding your breath. Sound also has a critical vibrational effect on the body in opening up the energy centers, also known as *chakras*, and letting energy flow throughout your system. Simply put, sound moves energy. Moving energy equals orgasm/s. Orgasms equal pleasure. Yee-ha!

Latihan

One of the techniques you'll use in Tantra in order to learn the self-generation of pleasure is called *Latihan*. Latihan is a meditation technique from the Subud (an Indonesian religious group). Latihan means "following inner guidance".

In Latihan, you stand silently and "open" to existence. Energy flows through you, taking any form, such as laughing, dancing, singing, crying.

Anything can happen. Some people refer to it as *authentic movement*. That's what I think of as the physical goal in all this, throwing away those preconceived notions of sex and love-making and just hanging around in the unknown, authentically being in your body.

How? That's what this book will teach you. But if you want to start somewhere, start with this:

Push the Red Button

Set aside at least ½ hour

Put on ethereal music, music that causes you to drift off

Stand blindfolded in a room where there is room for you to move around

Guided Imagery: Imagine yourself standing at the edge of a precipice. As you look over the edge, you see only darkness, the void. Notice that you are strapped into a harness. The harness is attached to a cable. The cable is attached to a zip line by a clasp. The zip line stretches across the void. Let go of your footing and allow yourself to swing out onto the zip line. Notice yourself dangling there over the unknown, the void. Feel yourself dangle. Then look up to notice a red button. This button can unfasten the clasp that attaches you to the zip line. Now, bravely reach up and push the red button.

Feel yourself falling fast, very fast into the unknown. Feel the wind on your face. Feel the wind through your hair as you fall.

Then almost as if the hands of Spirit have come to guide you, feel yourself floating as if there are feathers or a magic carpet has appeared to stop the fall. You find yourself now, floating in the unknown.

Allow yourself to move in the unknown following inner guidance. Only move when the impulse to move moves you. There are no prescribed steps, no prescribed postures. Allow movement to move you until the end of the music.

The more you practice this, the more you will be able to *Make Love in the Unknown* with your partner as described below.

Latihan for Two

A. Arrange to meet your partner regularly for extended and uninterrupted periods. (Your life probably isn't set up for this.

Making the commitment to spend valuable time on valuable love is the first step of all.)

B. Understand ahead of time that the energy can get intense, and not always pleasantly so. (Of course you want sex to be easy and effortless, and sometimes it just isn't. Accepting that might be the second step.)

C. Begin by meditating or sitting quietly together. Make your breathing as slow as possible. When you finally make love, the breathing will go fast and deep. Experience the contrasts between the two.

D. Have some opening ritual in order to prepare the space and honor each other. This can be anything that feels meaningful and relaxing to you. You want to worship your partner, and let your partner worship you. Perhaps face each other totally naked and touch each other's feet, or put garlands of flowers there. Maybe feed each other a piece of chocolate or offer a bit of wine. (I like to place red carnation petals on my partner's chakras.) Then gaze into each other's eyes for a good long while.

E. Worship brings the energy into focus. Now the man becomes a god and the woman becomes a goddess. Now your 'flawed' humanity is irrelevant, your name irrelevant. You are just pure energy. The whole attitude becomes so sublime that "you" disappear. Only in this moment should you begin making love. It has to be real, no pretending, no faking.

F. To be real, to fake nothing, move only when the impulse to move moves you. Don't worry about what impulse moves your partner. (Of course you want your partner to be the same as you. Letting go of that need and expectation might be the third step.) Allow your body to do what your body does without evaluating or judging. Just be present in the now, again and again. Mind will interfere, but your body knows what to do. Listen to it. When thoughts come about how you're going to pay the bills or what you might look like as you move, tell the thoughts to come back later, and sink into your body again.

G. Close your eyes and relax. There is nothing to do, nowhere to get to. You do not need a release. You do not need to be "taken" to some place by someone else. You are free to simply be. It is inside of this "be-ing" that love-making takes place. Move slowly during this practice, touching each other's bodies like a musical instrument. Let things grow. If you bring your mind into it, you'll notice that feeling disappears. Just go back to the body. Suddenly both your energies will rise together. Sometimes one of you will lead while the other follows, and this may shift all through your session.

H. Surrender to whatever is taking place. Feel the energy descending upon you and let it have its movement. Sometimes you will scream or moan, or your body will go into spontaneous postures or spasms. Nothing is taboo or inhibited. You can be as wild or as gentle as you give yourself permission to be. You don't have to direct it; simply let the energies meet and part and meet.

I. It's through your allowing it all that this is happening. If you want it to stop, just stop. You don't have to fear going out of control. You'll find that the experience is like making love with your whole body, rather than connecting only through the genitals.

It is important to note here again that Tantra is not fragmented, but all-encompassing. You cannot practice Tantra unless you create a situation in which it can be created. When you want to make love, make sure you have enough time. It shouldn't be done in a hurry or done as 'work' or a series of exercises with some sort of goal in mind. It's like a flower, blossoming in the proper environment with the proper conditions you have set up, through the water, light and nourishment you bring to it.

Making love in this way, you will tap into the most powerful life force. If you meditate and then worship each other, everything will be in alignment, coming from a high energetic vibration. You'll attain a peak orgasm you have never before known.

Often there is no ejaculation for the male, but orgasm will be there nonetheless. You may achieve a great orgasm in which the whole body throbs and pulsates, and this can cleanse your whole being.

Michael: Given the intention for making love in the unknown, it is possible that all that is not love may show up for healing and releasing, to be dealt with in order to allow for more freedom of self-expression during love-making. Luckily, you teach us how to deal with all the rest of it, so we do heal and we do release, and the result is not only making love in the unknown, but living life there as well.

And that is precisely the point! In Tantra, when two people are making love, if you are both non-selves, nothingness (or unrecognizable as who you were before), then orgasm just happens. You don't have to expend effort. Your body energy, your whole being loses its separate ego identity. Then you're no longer yourselves – you've fallen into the void, *bliss and ecstasy.*

With the kind of openness Tantra fosters, sometimes you can just look at each other and orgasm happens. Maybe only for moment upon moment, but the moments feel timeless. Anything can happen! That's living in the unknown. That's making love Tantra style, forcing nothing, being open to everything. It's making love in the unknown. It's what I'm hoping to teach you in this book. Now that we've had the rich, sumptuous dessert, it's time for the appetizers and the main course.

In this chapter, I've outlined *Law X: Make Love in the Unknown.*

You've learned:

- Sexual energy is life energy.

- The Big O-not just an orgasmic sex life, but a totally orgasmic life.

- Techniques for expanding orgasm in women.

- Techniques for expanding orgasm in men.

- The importance of breathing and making noise.

- Self-pleasuring prepares you for Tantric love-making.

- *Latihan* or authentic movement is the gateway to love-making in the Unknown.

Now let's look at *Tantric Law of Intimacy #1, Be Your Own Witness.* I will show you how to begin meditating on the way to deep spiritual growth and development Tantra style.

Law I
Be Your Own Witness

JUST ONE QUALITY of the Buddha has to be remembered. He consists only of one quality: witnessing. This small word witnessing contains the whole of spirituality. Witness that you are not the body. Witness that you are not the mind. Witness that you are only a witness. As the witnessing deepens, you start becoming drunk with the divine. That is what is called ecstasy.

– Osho

B*eing Your Own Witness* involves seeing yourself clearly, without judgment. Being Your Own Witness teaches you to see yourself as you really are. In fact, it means simply noticing what you're doing. To be your own witness is to become aware – aware, for example, of the never-ending story you're telling yourself about your life all the time, just under the surface of your awareness. In Tantra you learn to witness what you think and witness what you say. You learn that you are neither your mind, nor your body, nor your emotions. Why is this esoteric-sounding concept so important? Awareness marks the beginning of the end of the "automatic" you. Noticing and interrupting your automatic responses creates a gap between the on-going narrative you construct about yourself and your life – you know, the thing you call "just the way I am" – and who you *really* are, in the spiritual sense. Witnessing will show you your authentic self. Becoming that authentic self is what will allow true intimacy into your life.

Change! Wait, Don't Change!

It's a funny thing about being human that, although you want to change, part of you doesn't want anything to change. There's such comfort in it all being the way you're used to it being, even if that way is a lousy and miserable way. Be aware that only part of you wants happiness and love. The other part of you is terrified and holding on for dear life to every bad habit and destructive thought you have ever had. Oh well! You might as well just shrug and accept it, this fearful mind tells you.

Kay says, I remember being really angry with my husband for a long time. I had all these good reasons to be angry with him, and I went over and over the reasons in my head, almost every day.

One night, though, as we were getting ready for bed, I sort of stepped outside myself for a second and saw what I was doing. I saw that I was hoarding my resentment and shoring myself up against him. I was making myself feel strong, so that he couldn't hurt me again. At the same time, I was making our marriage a cold and lonely place, where nothing he did could please me, and also I was never pleased.

Oh my God, I thought, I'm doing to him what Dad used to do to Mom! For the first time I realized that my dad must have been scared. It took all my courage to do it, but that night I turned to James and told him what I had been doing, and that I was sorry. I was so ashamed. I was also scared to let it go. I saw that, too. If I let it go, he might get close to me again, and then our whole relationship would be different. Yes, I wanted it to be different, but I was also scared of it changing. Underneath everything, I was afraid of the intimacy.

Fear and Craving

Everyone has the need for love, and the need to hide that need, that vulnerability. The craving for and fear of intimacy is something that unites every human being on the planet. You handle that fear and craving in different ways. Some ways work and some drive the people you love fleeing from you in horror and self-preservation.

There's a complicating factor as well. Women and men have opposing needs when it comes to sex and relationship: As a woman, you're afraid you'll be left and have to manage everything on your own. As a man, you're afraid you'll have to leave just to have some autonomy.

As a woman, you'll give sex to get love, and as a man you'll give love to get sex. Now try to get along! You come to intimacy with such different fears that you are bound to work at cross-purposes, even when you're determined that THIS time you'll tell the truth and THIS time it'll be different. Even when you love each other, you end up feeling unappreciated, resentful, and lonely.

Intimacy with another requires, first and foremost, coming to peace with your own emotional and physical needs. This is not a small task, but it is a crucial one. It takes time and courage and forgiveness, coming from you, to you. If you want a sexually electric and truly intimate love affair, you have to begin unblocking and unleashing the sex force that is already inside you.

I know, I know, that's a tall order. And a very scary one. I'll get to the How-To further on, I promise.

Being your own witness starts small. You can probably observe yourself now, but can you observe yourself *without judgment*? Can you watch yourself and the thoughts running through your mind right now, and not condemn them or yourself? Ha! Didn't think so.

But not to worry. Everyone in the world has thoughts they don't really mean, fantasies, dreams, wishes, which are just that, not real. So why take them so seriously. If you dwell on them, you are only giving them power. Don't beat yourself up for the simple wish for five minutes to yourself when everyone around you seems to be doing nothing but making more demands on you. Or for being angry at your partner for forgetting your birthday.

If you just let these thoughts go, they will waft away like a feather on a breeze, here one second, gone the next. Let them arise, observe them, embrace them and then let them go with your exhale.

You'll get the hang of it the more you practice. The more you practice the more you'll see the benefits, and the benefits are quite noticeable, I promise. You'll feel more peaceful, more tolerant, more aware of the rich world that has nothing to do with doing, and everything to do with being.

Opinion Addiction

Being your own witness is going to show you all your millions of opinions and judgmental observations about other people. You'll begin to see how addicted you are to thinking you know the way the world works or should work, how fixated you are on your ideas and expectations. You'll start tuning in to your endless opinions about yourself and your worth, and the worth of other people. Like you really know what's going on for other people! Like it's really any of your business!

I know (because I'm the same way, and so is everyone else) that you think your opinions are really, really important. You even think they're somehow The Truth. You learned early to differentiate between good and bad, cheap and expensive, worthy and unworthy, pretty and ugly. You learned to be judgmental.

Being judgmental is fun and seductive because when you judge other people you get to feel superior, and feeling superior is just the bomb, isn't it? Of course, being judgmental starts on the outside, but it grows inward. You don't realize that all your judgments are going to come back one day and bite you right in the ass, but honey, they will.

Being your own witness will show you that for every judgment you have about someone else, you have ten for yourself. As unforgiving as you are of other people's mistakes, you are even less forgiving of your own. In fact, being your own witness is going to show you that in your secret mind you can do no right. Neither can anyone else. In your secret mind, no one's a winner. Not you, not anyone. Unless you've done some work on yourself, and I mean of the spiritual variety, all you can really see, as far as the horizon in every direction, is what's wrong with the world. Wrong with yourself. You can't experience openness with this closed view of the world and how you think it *should* work. In Tantra there is no *should*, there only IS.

The Cure

There's only one antidote to this kind of critical, judgment, and that is compassion. The point of being your own witness is to develop some compassion for yourself. But before you get there, you have to first look and see – really see – how much compassion you don't have.

I read something by Nina Utne (from the *Utne Reader* family), saying that compassion requires the grace of opening the heart. To have compassion, it is necessary to soften your heart to what you most hate and most fear. What a concept! Pick the thing you hate most, and look at it from a different angle. Instead of just reacting to it blindly, look at it from behind your witnessing eyes. See what there is to see. It takes courage and fortitude to do this, but do it anyway. Be brave. What is there for you to learn? Behind your automatic, knee-jerk, self-protecting response, what are you refusing to admit? What are you keeping out? What are you afraid of?

Being your own witness is letting those thoughts go rather than following them to their bitter end. It's taking an unflinching look at what's really going on within your mind simply witnessing the thoughts rather than looking with a harsh critical view. It's all about compassion. You might think that being hard on yourself will make you a better person, but more growth will happen under the gentle light of loving kindness than the glare of a spotlight on all the self-proclaimed "faults" you usually identify with.

Compassion arises when you can observe all that is happening inside and outside, and then consciously let the judgment go. Compassion in action leaves you free to choose your responses, rather than live at the mercy of your reactions. How? It happens naturally when you spend enough time getting quiet in your mind through meditation. Get quiet, get centered, and simply observe yourself. I guarantee, it'll be an eye-opening and heart-opening experience.

The Lizard Lives

A word about what is sometimes called *reptile brain* might be in order before I continue. Reptile brain is the primitive part of your gray matter, the part that's here to ensure your survival. When you feel threatened, reptile brain takes over, and reptile brain is not a sweet, warm, rational creature.

Reptile brain reacts to threat instantaneously. It doesn't have time to differentiate small threats from big ones, nor real ones from imaginary. Reptile brain wants to kill, wants to squash, will hide if it has to, and is determined to win at all costs. I'll repeat that last thing: It wants to win *at all costs*. It does not dare show an open, vulnerable side. Love, trust, and intimacy mean nothing when life is at stake, and reptile brain thinks your life is at stake every time you get rattled.

Make no mistake, though; reptile brain is crucial to your survival. It's gotten you this far, after all. But now that you want peace, happiness, good loving, maybe even some kind of spirituality in your life, reptile brain is causing a fair amount of trouble. When you're threatened, reptile brain uses every weapon in its arsenal against the people you love. That is, it uses the past, it uses threats, it uses your sadness, your failures, your partner's failures, even sex and rejecting sex as a weapon. Reptile brain is a destroyer of happiness, and intimacy.

So what do you do with it? Own up to it and embrace it, of course. This is Tantra, after all, where there is no light without dark. You don't reject any part of yourself in Tantra. There's no getting rid of your shadow anyway, there's only coming to peace with it. The way you begin doing that is by being your own witness.

Reptile Rage

I remember once being my own witness during a fight with a colleague. I made what I thought was a very simple request of him. I didn't think it was extraordinary or that it would cause undue pain. For whatever reason, though, he couldn't hear it. So I rephrased the request in a couple of different ways, and when I saw that he just couldn't receive it, I got quiet and went into the witness. The quieter I became, the louder he became, and the more he raged.

I kept noticing this and got even quieter. It's not like I wanted to torment him, but there seemed to be nothing else I could say. Yet the less I said the more he "went off", so to speak.

While I was witnessing this process, I realized that I was watching myself in a previous relationship. In that relationship, though, the roles were reversed – I was the angry one and my partner was me. I remembered my ex-lover getting quieter and quieter, watching me as I ranted and raved. That's what my colleague was doing now, ranting and raving, completely unreachable. From the position of witness, I watched with amazement. I was fascinated! I could hardly tear myself away, but then I had to. It was obviously doing no good to keep going around and around. When I left the conversation, I was calm, and I knew that his rage was his; it had nothing to do with me. Previously, I would have gotten completely involved in the fight. This time, no. Thank goodness for the witness!

Tune In

To be your own witness doesn't require action. You don't have to *do* anything. You only have to be aware. You only have to notice. This is not so easy though, certainly not at first. Here's how it works:

Start by closing your eyes and noticing your feelings, almost as if from a distance. Notice what you are sensing in your body. Visit the base of your spine and notice. Move to your sex area and notice.

When I say notice, see what your senses are telling you, bring your conscious awareness to the specific area and take note. Are you tight, loose, hot, cold? Do you feel tingly sensations or swirling? Are you not feeling anything? Are you numb?

Notice your belly and solar plexus. Are you feeling a big block here or tightness, restriction?

Then move up to your heart. Notice if it heavy or light. Does it feel expansive or shut tight?

Then notice in your throat. Is it constricted or restricted? Swallow and see what you feel there.

Notice the area between your eyebrows. Is there tension there? Do you see colors when your eyes are closed or do you just see blackness?

Now notice the area above the top of your head and around it, the area that would be your halo. Do you feel open and in touch with the energy here or are you aware of a cloud over your head?

Now notice when judgment comes in. Notice when anger comes. Notice when fear rises up, and notice how you normally would respond.

Notice when someone's behavior sets off a knee-jerk response in you. Notice in your body when you want to fight or run, or when you can't do anything but freeze. Notice everything. Just notice. Just be aware. That's all.

You might take a moment right now and experience *being your own witness*. This is what you do: Take a deep, calming breath. Look at yourself – at the processing going on inside – as if you were half a loving step away. Now listen to yourself, to what your inner voice is saying. You can even watch yourself watching yourself. There's a lot going on in the mind and many layers to it. Get in the habit of observing your mind at work.

The Body Never Lies

You can guide yourself through this if you'd like, if you need help tuning in. If it's murky to you what you're feeling, start like this: "I notice that my body is feeling _____. The part of my body that seems most affected is my _____. When I focus in on that body part, I have _____ sensations. I notice I began feeling these sensations _____ when _____ happened."

OK, now sit with that for a minute. Watch yourself experiencing your sensations and/or emotions. You may be surprised when you discover the event that actually set you off and where you wind up feeling it in your body. You'll be tempted to deny or dismiss this, but the body never lies. Your mind can play all kinds of games, and boy does it, but the body never lies. Learn to trust it. Some people call this "coming to your senses".

You are also growing more in tune with your energy centers, and your aura that you project on the world. Your belly, your heart, your forehead are all sending you messages. In training yourself in this union of mind, body and spirit, you will learn to trust your intuition, your inner guidance that is sourced in the body.

As you go through your day, be aware of when your moods shift and how your body reacts. Bring in the witness, especially when you're upset. Breathe in through your nose, and exhale deeply out your mouth. If you can, make a sighing sound as you exhale. When you're ready, look at yourself again, gently, and continue asking yourself questions about what is going on. Remember that whatever you're doing in this moment, you can always stop. You can stop, breathe, and be aware. That's all it takes to break a cycle of behavior. Did you know that? If you feel you are being affected badly by another's negative energy, as in the story I told about my raging colleague, you can just puff air out of your nostrils in little bursts to dispel the residue.

Follow and respect your own process. Watch it, notice it, and look carefully at it. Ask yourself these questions, and let the answers come bubbling up on their own without editing: "Notice that a small thing triggered a large reaction." "What is it reminding me of?" "When else did I feel this way?" You might think you're behaving irrationally, but you aren't. You might be reacting in this moment to something that happened a long time ago, but you're not being irrational. After all, the psyche is unaware of the passage of time. Just as you are unaware of the triggers which are causing you to act in this way until you begin to act as your own witness.

Watch and Grow

Why would you want to commit to this constant vigil? The answer is simple. By being mindful and aware, acting as your own witness, you eventually empower yourself to make choices in life that suit you, rather than feeling thrown about willy-nilly and bewildered by circumstances.

You become conscious. You have the freedom to choose. You act, rather than react. You let yourself learn in every aspect and area of your life that you don't need to push for growth, neither in yourself, nor in your lover. Growth is natural. Force is unnecessary. Witnessing is enough.

The witness practice, which is the cornerstone of all meditation, develops and deepens the more you do it. It becomes easier with practice. Over time, this is a tremendous form of empowerment. Simply witnessing your own mind will change your relationships, and witnessing yourself as you go through the processes and practices in this book will add immensely to your experience.

Think of the witness as your friend, your most constant companion. Learn all you can about it, come to know it intimately. Bring it in whenever you can. Keep practicing the skill, especially in times of crisis/opportunity, when your reptile brain is in high gear. Say hello to your scaly friend, or watch it operating for a while if you want. It's not going anywhere. Just keep witnessing and keep breathing. If you can step back and observe yourself even once in the midst of an emotionally charged situation, you'll see your whole history with different eyes. *Be your own witness* and you'll be in charge of your own life.

The Witness, and Your Sexuality

Being our own witness is always the most difficult in the context of our own sexuality. Notions of right and wrong, good and bad, normal versus abnormal, torment us almost from the moment we become aware of our gender. And what society expects us to do, be, think as a result of that gender.

The beauty of Tantra is that there is no expectation. The beauty of *being your own witness* is that there is no judgment. Fantasies, desires, all are acceptable, for they are just that, mere acts of the mind. They have no more solidity than a soap bubble. And therefore they are nothing to worry about. As vivid you think your imagination is, and as depraved as you might think you are, believe me, other people have had the exact same thoughts and fantasies. Anyone who claims they never masturbate is a liar.

Tantra is about telling the truth. All of it. It's about being open. Through the witness, you can just observe, and thus be open to all the pleasure you've longed for, if you allow yourself to have it.

In this chapter on *Tantric Law I, Being Your Own Witness,* you've learned:

- How your fear of change stifles intimacy and spiritual growth.

- How being your own witness (meditating) fosters your spiritual growth.

- How the *reptile brain* tries to stop you from growing.

- How you can overcome your *reptile brain* through practicing witness meditations.

- How you can tune into your thoughts and let them go.

- How you can tune into your body as a reflection of your mind and emotions.

- How your inner witness can open you up to your own sexuality.

In the next chapter, *Tantric Law II, Please Yourself,* I will show you how you can allow your own witness to focus on your most vulnerable inner self, your sexual self, and bring it out into the light of bliss.

Law II
Please Yourself

And in the end, the love you take is equal to the love you make.

— The Beatles

To the turned on woman, everything her partner does will seem inspired and creative. Turned on, our partners are heroes before they even walk through the door.

— Patricia Taylor

Be warned. All notions of political correctness are about to go out the window. Men and women are not from different planets, we are all on the same one, but hopeless at communicating with each other, because, as I discussed in Law I, *Being Your Own Witness,* we are failures at communicating truthfully even with ourselves. In this chapter, it is going to seem that I am attacking women. So, in advance, I want you to know that I feel the survival of our planet rests in women's ability to reclaim their power. I believe in my heart it is women's job and fate and privilege to rescue the world, but as you will see, I think there is a huge gap between where they are, and where they have to be in order for this to happen. In this chapter I attempt to give the impetus to close the gap even if it makes you mad.

In my courses, I have had a panel of men sit in front of the room for a question-answer session from the women. The men were always asked, "What do you want from women?"

Invariably they would agree: "Tell us exactly what you want." If women would just be straight about that, they'd say, it would be so much easier to figure things out! No doubt this is true, but how can women answer this?

Only through your inner witness can you come to some sort of understanding of what will please you most. And only when you are pleased yourself can you ever hope to share the gift of true pleasure with a partner.

What Women Want

Women want men to make them happy. But what does that mean? Women don't know what they want. The closest a woman can come to an answer is to say, "Don't leave. Don't go off to war, to work, to be with and impregnate other women."

But that's not really the answer.

Do you know what they really want? They want their power and security back. They want to be beautiful in their own eyes. They want safety on their own terms. They want to be empowered.

The truth is, men can't give them these things. No one can. Women have to give it to themselves – and yet they don't know how.

Consequently, a lot of women are miserable. I'm sorry, but it's true. In this age of post women's liberation, you're miserable and - here comes the inflaming part - you're waiting around for men to make you happy. It's been a long wait already, so don't hold your breath.

Men, you *cannot* make women happy - at least not in the way women think you should. Women, you have to source your own pleasure and, frankly, you're pretty bad at it.

Oh, Princess?

In your heart of hearts, you women are bitter and disappointed because the men in your lives have failed to make your dreams come true. Either Daddy made you feel special and safe and no one else has ever managed to, or Daddy let you down and so has every man since. No self-respecting woman wants to admit this, of course (least of all me), but just about everything you're doing is geared to getting a man, then getting the man to hurry up and turn you into the princess you were always meant to be.

But men, you dirty dogs, have you noticed (according to women) you can't get the job done right? No matter what you do, it's not good enough?

Hey, women, what if you're miserable not because of your man, but because long ago you gave away your power to men, and now you think the only way you can get power back is by having a man to control, or by acting like a man yourself?

I told you this was inflammatory. You think you're too modern and evolved for this kind of game. Well, stick around I might convince you yet. I happen to know that lots of women have found it easier to stop relating to men altogether rather than deal with the painful truth that they are unwilling, or unable, to own their own power.

Be Careful What You Ask For

For men these days it goes something like this: Your woman demands that you be more sensitive. You resist at first, being a man, but eventually you oblige. (After all, being a man, you want your woman to be happy.)

So you get sensitive and "new-aged" and interested in the color of the kitchen tile and in pushing the baby stroller. You change, move away from your masculine self, and guess what? It doesn't work. Your woman STILL isn't happy!

Part of the problem is that your new sensitivity stops you from being the masculine animal she still needs you to be, especially in bed. Now your woman is bitching and moaning (secretly or openly) that you're not enough of a man. Is this helpful?

No. This causes you to flounder even more. You've become too sensitive to tell her to go to hell and get her ass to bed, which is what she needs to hear, and too sensitive to ravish her once she gets there, which is what she really needs you to do.

Here's the picture in many pairings I've seen in my workshops: The woman is seething, the man is lost and miserable, and the whole relationship has become a blame game and succumbed to a peculiar modern condition that *Newsweek* (in June of 2003) called DINS – Double-Income-No-Sex couples. Married people aren't "doing it" anymore; even the ones without kids! What the heck is up with that (or not UP!)? Well, I know what's up with that, and I know the solution. Stay tuned.

Shiva Shakti Male Female Homo Hetero

While you are still reeling from my outrageous statements, this might be a good time to say something about same-sex couples and gender in general. In Tantra, one of the things you'll work with is getting to know the male and the female side of yourself and your partner.

The male energy is called Shiva; female energy is called Shakti. Everyone is made up of both, in varying amounts. If you're a man with a lot of Shiva energy, you'll feel the lack of Shakti and go looking for a woman to supply it. If you're a gay man with a lot of Shiva energy, you'll look for a man who has a lot of Shakti energy to make up for your lack.

If you're a woman who's somewhat masculine, whether on the inside or out, you're probably going to match up with a man who's somewhat feminine, to balance you out. It's interesting to me that gays and lesbians are often aware of their category-within-a-category. If you're femme or butch, top or bottom, you probably know it already. Straight folks can be a little confused (and defensive) when told they have both aspects within them.

Forget your defensiveness. This out-of-balance state is what fuels the quest for love, for heteros and homos and everyone in between. What you're looking for in a mate is your other polarity – your other half, so to speak. The more extreme the polarities, the more turned on you are. The more muted the polarities, the less desire you feel. It's as simple as that!

The polarities are not fixed, but change with age, hormones, stress at work, and other factors, but generally speaking, you will tend more towards one than the other.

In Tantra, you learn to balance your own male and female polarities, enabling you to be in a sacred union with the Shiva/Shakti energy inside you. Then you have new choices – you can play with a broader palette for desirability's sake or you can remain in the center, your two selves merged, and feel more whole and in total love with yourself. It's up to you.

By the way, this is Tantra, and there's nothing wrong or right about masculine and feminine, whatever your gender. Tantra isn't a test of your manhood or your desirability as a woman. It's a path toward becoming aware of what you're manifesting and whether it's working for you and your partner. Your energy affects your partner, after all, just as your partner's energy affects you, especially when it's an unconscious pull, like the force of gravity. There is no right or wrong with gravity, no judgment. It simply is.

The Masculine and the Feminine

In general, we can attribute certain characteristics to Shiva and Shakti.

Shiva (Male) qualities:

Left-brained
Rational
Analytical
Light
Heaven
Death
Controlled
Mind
Giving
Outside
Logical
Forcing

Shakti (Female) qualities:

Right-brained
Emotional
Intuitive
Dark
Earth
Birth
Chaotic
Body
Receiving
Inside
Inner Guiding
Allowing

Male Energy, Female Energy, and Pleasing Yourself

Women, you have been conditioned to disregard your own pleasure signals in favor of others'. Many men do it too. If you're the one in the relationship who tends to the needs of others *over your own*, you might be playing the role of victim. As a victim you feel that others have all the power to choose, and you have none. Feeling powerless leads to a chronic blaming of others for how your life is turning out. That's no good for you, and it's no good for them.

So what's the solution? First you breathe, deep, anchoring breaths. Then, witness your relationship role, and witness your reaction. When you can focus clearly again, think long and hard about what it would take to *Please Yourself.*

Why? Because what pleases you is your guiding light, showing you the way forward. It's how you find and follow your bliss. When you are manifesting primarily your Shakti energy, finding and following your own bliss can be hard to do.

So what pleases you? This is a serious question. Learn to allow pleasure into your life anywhere, and it will affect all the other parts of your life. Expand your pleasure in the bedroom, and your life will expand in every direction. Expand your pleasure when you're eating dinner or walking down the street, and your capacity for pleasure and zest for living will expand. The key is awareness – pay attention to what pleases you. Then allow yourself to be pleased.

You're reading a book about transformational pleasure and intimacy, so of course I'm talking about deep joy, orgasmic bliss. I'm not talking about throw-away bits of time that only keep you masked from yourself, fleeing from your inner demons, rather than facing them head on and *being your own witness.* I'm not advocating spending your life in front of the TV, or medicating your inner pain and darkness by shoveling in liquor, food, and random sex.

Don't get me wrong, there are times when that stuff is just the ticket. You know if it's destructive or helpful - so tune in, not out, with the help of your inner witness. When you truly learn to please yourself, you won't have to numb out the world out of pain and resentment, but will engage with it on every level for the most blissfully full experiences of pleasure and joy.

How's This Working for You?

In a very basic way, you can look around and ask yourself an elemental question: Is what I'm doing working for me? It's not a trick question. There is no right or wrong answer here. And not a question that someone else can provide answers to for you, either.

Is what you're doing working for you? All the wisdom you need to answer that question is right inside your body. Find your center, your wise voice, and experiment with what feels pleasing to you, from the kind of shaving cream you use to the way you have sex. Stop yourself as many times a day as you can stand to, and ask, "Is this really what I want to be doing now?" Ask yourself, "Is this giving me pleasure?" You might even ask, "When I do this, do I feel empowered?" "Do I feel like jumping for joy?" These are important questions.

A good clue that you're not pleasing yourself is noticing the rage that engulfs you when other people around you are perfectly happy. They are pleasing themselves effortlessly and rather than be happy for them, you want to stomp them into the ground.

Hello - reptile brain is trying to tell you something. It's telling you to please *yourself*. Focusing on other people is just a tricky way of avoiding change, of keeping things as they are - with you unfulfilled and feeling like a victim. Listen to that inner message. It is telling you that you get to be happy in this life. You do.

> Amy says: The concept *Please Yourself* has made the biggest difference to me. It was the one I clung to immediately after the Ecstasy course. I made sure to take home a drumming CD to dance to. Whenever I started feeling the old familiar low energy, negative thinking mentality, I stopped myself, put on that CD, and started pumping and squeezing the pubococcgeal (PC) muscles. Soon I would feel like dancing, and I'd really get the energy going. That would pick me up and satisfy me, and I could approach my day from a much more productive standpoint. It was a new awareness to understand that there was something I could do to stay positive, to not let worry get me down.

Pleasure Hunt

In my courses, I lead a lot of exercises designed to teach women how to make themselves happy. Often in these exercises men "hold the space" while women look to see what they really want.

Note to men: Holding the space for the woman in your life means standing tall and strong in the face of her rage and grief. You, as the male partner, are not required either to provide the answers for your woman or to yield to her moods even though she demands this of you. You will help her most by staying true to yourself (a Shiva quality), and simply holding the space, breathing, and maintaining *your own witness*.

Note to women: Eventually you will discover that you can give pleasure to yourself. You are allowed to start small. Wherever you drop the pebble in, ripples will spread. Begin adding pleasure to your day. Take time actively to choose the color of your lipstick, the movies you watch, the kind of tea you drink. Choose the small things that please you and it will become easier to choose the large things. Stop a few times every day and ask, "Is this really giving me pleasure?" and "Is this really what I want?" You might be surprised by the answer. You will certainly be strengthened by the process. See, here's another inflammatory truth: When the woman is happy, everyone else is free to be happy. It's just one of those things. A happy Shakti is a happy family. An unhappy Shakti is misery for all.

In Tantra – and as you read this book – you will come to recognize when your male side or your female side is dominant. There's nothing you need to do about it in any active sense. But by being your own witness and learning to please yourself, you will eventually let yourself choose the pattern and gender aspect that will serve you best at any given time. One tip I can give you is that in order to build passion you must have an intense polarity between lovers.

You, as a woman, may be a big executive inhabiting the male polarity of power by day. But by night, turn yourself into the most feminine creature you can imagine, if you want passion in the bedroom.

You, as a man may be the most sensitive caretaker the world has ever seen; you've been given the Alan Alda award for sensitivity. But if you want hot, hot sex, you must beat your chest like Tarzan and act like a caveman. To both of you – find the answer to pleasing yourself in your extreme feminine or masculine polarities when you want passion in bed. Just try, for gosh sakes! Remember our deliciously decadent opening dessert, Tantric Law X, – *make love in the unknown*. See if you can have fun with this.

Pleasing yourself will go a long way toward curing a passionless life and relationship. Why? Because every one of us, in our hearts, is passionate. If you're shaking your head and saying, "Not me," or "Not my lover," it's not because the passion isn't there. It's because the passion has been squashed down. You've neglected your pleasure. There are a million reasons you've done this – all of them good ones and most of them self-protective.

But guess what? It's time for something else now. Probably you've neglected your pleasure for a long time. Maybe such a long time that you fear it is too late. But that was the past. Observe it as a witness, learn your lessons from it, then let it go. That was then, this is now. Being in the present is what Tantra is all about.

Instead of neglecting your deep joy, you know you can grow it. Here's a great idea: Instead of DINS, let's have DIDS (Double Income Double Sex)! Let's turn the tide! Find ways to *Please Yourself* and your passion will fuel your life *and* your relationships, leading to the next of the Tantric Laws of Intimacy, Law III: *Emotional Release.*

In *Tantric Law II: Please Yourself,* you learned:

- You are responsible for your own pleasure.

- Sizzling sex and passion is based on the polarity of sexual energy between masculine and feminine.

- We all possess both masculine and feminine energies.

- The general characteristics of each of these energies.

- You use being your own witness to allow yourself to play with the energies and make yourself happy.

- Understanding the nature of your sexual energy is the gateway to bliss.

Law III
Emotional Release

All that this world needs is a good cleansing of the heart of all the inhibitions of the past. And laughter and tears can do both. Tears will take out all the agony that is hidden inside you and laughter will take all that is preventing your ecstasy. Once you have learned the art you will be immensely surprised.

– Osho

As soon as people purge and process the feelings of hurt or anger, they are freed up to experience joy, pleasure and open expression without fear.

– Dr. Judy Kuriansky

Well, here we are at the Third Law, and finally we're getting to the body. I love the body, and I always did. True, I might have wished for thinner thighs, and it did take me ten years to get through menopause, but I love my body.

In Tantra we say it's the mind that gets you stuck and the body that gets you unstuck. I firmly believe that everything you need to know is there inside that precious vessel you fill and empty all day long. Your memories are stored in the cells of your body. There is wisdom in your gut reactions. There is pleasure and pain and real knowledge all in your own wonderful body waiting to be tapped by you. Lucky you!

Body Beautiful

I'm glad you're reading this because I want you to experience the feeling of pleasure in your skin and muscles and bones and movement that I have experienced, and that people who go through my workshops all experience. This feeling has nothing to do with how you look, as in your appearance. It's a different experience of knowing when the body radiates from within.

Let me say it again: Your body is a wonderful thing, and you could put your hands on your heart right now and thank it for being there for you and doing the best job it can under the circumstances. Seriously, just put your hand over your heart and send a grateful message to yourself. Have you ever done that? It's lovely. Don't think you can't be self-loving because you aren't the person you want to be or don't have the body you think you should have. It actually works the opposite way; the more you love yourself, the more you'll come to be what you want to be.

Feelings

OK, now let's talk about your emotional life. You've found yourself somehow in adulthood, right? You're expecting yourself to behave like an adult, expecting to have your emotions completely handled and under control, right? At the same time you want to be in a relationship that's full of passion and deep intimacy. The problem is you don't know how to do both. How do you control your emotions and also *feel* your emotions? How do you have the right emotional response to things, and not go off the deep end at the smallest provocation?

Furthermore, when is it all right to cry? What if you can't cry? What if you can't stop crying once you start? What about anger? Oh boy, anger! Not to mention shame, oh boy, oh boy.

What do you do if you don't feel anything at all? I mean really, what if you're just plain numb? You may be reading this section and asking yourself, "What anger? What shame? What guilt?" Or maybe, "What tightness in the solar plexus? What shortness of breath?"

This chapter is for you, too. You might tell me that you can't feel anything, but my experience has taught me otherwise. You've felt so deeply, without any allowance for it, that you've had to put a lid on yourself in an effort to stop feeling those "dangerous" emotions anymore. Society tells men not to be sissies and not to feel, and sometimes parents can't deal with the anger or unhappiness of their children, so they just shut them down. If that happened to you and you took the message to heart, your emotions have been pushed so far inside you that you think you don't have them at all. But you do.

I've found in my courses that the very men who have kept a tight lid on their emotions – and those women who have become like men (not wanting to be "weak" or left behind) – burst full open during my second-level course, *Ecstasy*. As they do, they begin to feel alive again. When I say alive, I mean *excited* to be alive, not necessarily excited by stuff or possessions, but by breathing and feeling and being fully alive.

Pressure

What you feel in your body (as in your senses) is important because your senses are telling you when something is or isn't okay within you. Denying these feelings won't make them go away. Deny them and they'll hide in your body, waiting to ambush you when your guard is down. Next thing you know, your partner can do one thing wrong and you'll find yourself beside yourself, screaming in a complete fury, or locked down in a seven-day vow of silence, or even deciding never to have sex again as some kind of punishment. (Just think about it—who is *really* suffering when you resentfully withhold sex?) It's not the incident itself that has gotten you so worked up. It's the fact that you've been denying your emotions for so long that your body has filled up, the heat is on, and now the kettle has got to blow. When your internal pressure builds up too high, either you're going to dump your poison onto the people around you, or you're going to become self-destructive. If you don't have a safety valve, anger, hurt, and fear build up in the mind and memory, as well as in the body. The body suffers as a result, and so do you. By practicing *Emotional Release* instead, you can loosen up and burn off your emotional garbage in much the same way you'd use a gasoline conditioner to de-gunk your engine.

Alyce shared; "As a result of doing *Emotional Release* regularly, my life has an ease about it that I have never known before. It's a new feeling of lightness. In addition, I see that I now honor what others say by listening, whereas before, while they were talking, I would make them wrong in my mind because I did not agree with their opinions or actions. Now I find I am quiet in my mind when I listen."

How it Works

Emotional Release requires only two things: sound and movement. Sound moves energy. You're trying to move energy out of the locked places in your body. Movement moves energy as well. That's why regular exercise is crucial. It's not just that it burns calories; it also allows for emotional well-being. When energy releases in the body, you can feel it go. (Sometimes this practice is called *clearing* rather than *releasing*. I use the terms interchangeably.) Making sound enables you to release emotions and trapped energy you didn't even know were blocked.

If you've unconsciously been drawn to and picked a partner with whom you have ended up working out a lot of childhood issues, the emotional life of your relationship probably goes from very good to very bad a lot, up and down like the proverbial roller coaster. Roller coasters are fun to ride, but after a while you want off before you get sick. *Emotional Release* is a way off the ride.

Angie said, "Releasing emotions has proved itself in my relationship with my partner. The times I didn't clear the emotions first, speaking my truth didn't work. It came out wrong, hurtful to him. One time, practicing release in response to something else prompted a great intimate sharing with my partner."

Breathing and Squeezing

At the most basic level, releasing your emotions is just a matter of stomping your feet and screaming yourself tired, or going some place safe to cry yourself empty. *Emotional Release* is an adult's version of temper tantrums and crying jags. (See how wise children are?)

If you don't want to scream and cry, though, you can practice with deep sighing, loud shouting, or grunting. Moaning is good, too. I'm emphasizing making different kinds of sounds here because, as I said earlier, sound moves energy, and this is what allows for the blocked emotions to be released. So it's very important to make some sound, any sound.

In order to do Tantric *Emotional Release*, first it's necessary to learn the Tantric *Breathe and Squeeze*. This is a basic breathing technique designed to root you in your body and get your energy flowing. From the root chakra (more about that in a moment) you bring energy up to fill the whole body with the vital life force, vibrant sexual energy.

I'm going to teach you to do this basic part first; later in the chapter I'll show you how to use it to do full-fledged *Emotional Release*. Here's how you do the Tantric *Breathe and Squeeze*:

A) Make sure you are sitting straight either in a chair or on the floor. Start squeezing your pelvic and rectal muscles rhythmically. Just do this a few times until you get a nice and steady beat going, not too fast.

B) Once you have the rhythm, coordinate your exhale with the squeezing. Every time you squeeze the butt and sex muscles exhale with the sound "choo." It's like a sneezing sound of "ah choo," but only the "choo" part. So when the muscles are squeezed you are making the sound "choo" at the same time. (This may take a little getting used to because the mind often wants to do something else here.)

    Do it ten or twenty times right now, and feel your body come alive. Really squeeze those muscles. It's such a good feeling to fully wake your body up.

C) The next step is to change "choo" to another sound. You can start with an easy sound, "Ha! Ha! Ha! Ha!" Do this over and over loudly while continuing to squeeze.

D) Finally, take in a deep breath through the nose. Tighten every muscle in the body including feet, hands, arms, shoulders, butt, face – everything. Hold your breath while all your muscles are tight. Take a little sniff through the nose. Then exhale through the mouth while making a sound like a very big sigh of relief. Do this three times. Make as much noise as you like.

E) Now keep your eyes closed and notice how you feel. Most likely, you will find yourself invigorated and relaxed at the same time.

The Tantric *Breathe and Squeeze* is a lifesaver, possibly literally. Even without the tantrum, you can breathe and feel rejuvenated. If you're trying to lose weight, do it a few times before you eat, or a few times afterwards. If you're feeling sleepy at the wrong time, do it to wake yourself up. When you think you're going to lose it with the kids or your lover, *breathe and squeeze* instead.

In fact, you can even use this practice when you're going to have sex. That's right, this is **a sex technique**, so pay attention! If you want to feel charged up, breathe and squeeze gently while getting ready for bed. If you're already feeling romantic, do it together during foreplay, or during penetration. This one simple technique will significantly increase the sexual pleasure of both partners. In fact, the Tantric *Breathe and Squeeze* is one of the most useful tools I can offer you to increase sexual pleasure, and cause you to be present in the moment.

Chakras

I want to digress a little here to introduce the concept of *Chakras* and give you an understanding of what occurs during Tantric *Emotional Release*. Chakra is the Sanskrit word meaning "wheel" or "vortex". There are seven main chakras, or energy centers shaped like three dimensional flat spirals in the body, located at various points along the spine from the coccyx to above the top of the head. Each chakra has a different purpose, and each chakra can be opened or closed, depending on what's going on in your life or what went on before.

In Tantra there are many breathing exercises and postures designed to unblock the chakras. When you do the Tantric *breathe and squeeze*, you're activating the two lower chakras, the root and sex chakras where you store unconscious memories. *Emotional Release* is geared to empower you to release those memories that may be blocking you in your life even if you can't quite remember the incident. This makes it very powerful stuff because you can free yourself from the past without even having to talk about it, or even think about it!

As you read about the seven main chakras, listed below in order from the base of the spine upward, tune in to each part of your body and notice what you're sensing there, like loose or tight, tingly or numb, hot or cold. Also witness what you're telling yourself about that chakra area or the issues associated with it. Just notice.

First Chakra – Root

The first chakra is at the base of the spine and represents the *earth and physical identity. It's also called the root, and is oriented to self-preservation.* The root chakra deals with issues of early childhood, the life force, and our place in the family and society. It forms our foundation, if you will. Because it represents the earth element, it is related to our survival instincts, and to our sense of grounding and connection to our bodies on the physical plane.

Ideally this chakra brings us health, prosperity, and security. It's a very powerful, largely unconscious energy center, and in Tantra we activate it by squeezing the rectal and butt muscles. Granted, this may not be something you do every day, but by the end of this book it might be, and you won't even be embarrassed. Try squeezing and releasing there now. Isolate the small muscles around your anus and squeeze and release. Do it ten times, making sure to keep breathing.

Second Chakra – Sex

The second chakra is located in the abdomen, lower back, and sexual organs. It represents the element *water*. It is very powerful as it relates to largely unconscious issues of pleasure and pain. I have often said that it takes ten good experiences to counter one negative experience stored in the second chakra. Here is housed cellular memory related to our boundaries being trespassed, to violation, embarrassment, humiliation, romantic love or rejection, and our creativity. It connects us to others through feeling desire.

Ideally this chakra brings us fluidity and grace, depth of feeling, sexual fulfillment, and the ability to accept change. We activate it by squeezing the pelvic and PC (pubococcygeal) muscles, something known to many women already as "doing Kegels," noted for increasing the pleasure of orgasm and strengthening the vaginal vault for childbirth. Men should also do this on a regular basis, as it strengthens the muscles of the penis and helps you to control ejaculation.

Note: The PC muscles are the ones both men and women use to stop and start the flow of urine. So if you are not sure where they are, the next time you go to the bathroom, try to stop and start and stop and start again your flow of urine, until you get a feel for them. Once you isolate the PC muscles, you'll be able to squeeze them any time you like to strengthen and tone them.

Third Chakra – Solar Plexus

The third chakra, known as the power center, is located in the upper abdomen at the solar plexus. "Solar" refers to the sun, an easy way to remember that this chakra is the source of our power out in the "real" world. When healthy, this chakra brings us energy, effectiveness, spontaneity, and non-dominating power. It rules our personal will and autonomy, as well as our metabolism. The energy we use to make business deals and negotiate contracts comes from the third chakra, and courage is also housed here.

This chakra is oriented to self-definition, and represents fire and ego identity. Positioned between the sex and heart chakras, people often put on extra weight here, which has the effect of numbing the connection – or creating a barrier – between sex and love. With the third chakra opened, it is easier to connect sexual desires to heart-based motivations.

These first three chakras work together to bring unconscious, sometimes painful experiences up to our conscious mind – often when we're having sexual relations! Did you ever have the experience of crying during love-making or wondering why your partner was crying? Sometimes you, as the wondering partner, think it's something you've said or done, but it probably has very little, if anything, to do with you. A painful experience from the past may be working its way up and out of the cellular memory bank.

Fourth Chakra – Heart

The fourth chakra is the heart chakra. It represents air, and is the source of love and unconditional caring about all beings and things. It is the integrator of opposites in the psyche: mind and body, male and female, persona and shadow, ego separateness and unity. It is also the place where the lower chakras and upper chakras meet, so it sources the union of the physical and the spiritual.

The heart chakra houses *social identity, and is oriented to self-acceptance and compassion.* Often our hearts feel heavy and weighted down, instead of feeling like they have wings.

An open and healthy fourth chakra allows us to love deeply and have a sense of peace and centeredness. I've noticed that although many people have open hearts, if they have not dealt with the shadows that dwell in the first three chakras, then their words and actions may seem inconsistent to others.

Fifth Chakra – Throat

The fifth chakra is located in the throat and represents sound and creative identity. It is oriented to self-expression. Here we experience the world symbolically through vibration, such as the vibration of sound representing language. This chakra deals with communication and with honestly sharing our intellectual ideas, feelings, values, and assessments. It also involves the courage to speak our truth in terms of creativity, feelings, intentions, and commitments. The fifth chakra has to do with declaration and keeping our word, plus uninhibited self-expression – setting intentions and manifesting them.

Sixth Chakra – Forehead

The sixth chakra is located in the center of the forehead and represents the element of light. This chakra is known as the brow chakra, or third eye center, and is related to the act of seeing, both physically and intuitively. Oriented to self-reflection, the third eye opens our psychic faculties and our understanding of the unconscious. When fully open, it allows us to see "the big picture" rather than seeing only what we want to see. In Eastern religions, the third eye is the eye of wisdom and insight.

Seventh Chakra – Crown

The seventh chakra floats above and around your head, the same place a halo would be seen. It is the chakra of transformation and enlightenment, representing thought and universal identity. It is oriented to true self-knowledge.

This chakra represents consciousness as pure awareness, or what we've come to call cosmic consciousness. It is our connection to the greater world beyond, to a timeless place of all-knowing. When fully open and developed, this chakra brings us knowledge, wisdom, understanding, spiritual connection, and bliss.

The Role of the Chakras in Emotional Release

One of the reasons Tantra is so amazing is that it deliberately uses the energy of the First and Second chakras (the Root and Sex chakras), where other spiritual practices do not. Transformation occurs easily in Tantra because subconscious memories stored at a cellular level in the lower chakras surface for conscious processing and letting go. This frees you from emotional toxins, allowing you to be in the present, to experience pleasure and live in the unknown (remember Law X: *Make Love in the Unknown?*) rather than be stuck the past.

In the present you can learn to move the energy of the root and sex chakras upwards, to open each chakra in turn, and then allow the energy to float back down. This is called *transmutation.* Spiritual enlightenment becomes possible as you learn to move your sexual energy up and down the chakras. In doing that, you bring earthly energy up to heaven, and then bring heavenly energy back to earth through *your* body. You can experience heaven on earth!

Tantric Emotional Release

There are lots of methods you can use to release your emotions safely: screaming in the car, hitting a punching bag, and simply crying and laughing all week. Here I'm going to share more structured ways of practicing emotional release. These methods take some preparation and time, and may seem pretty weird at first. They're probably not something you've been used to doing in your ordinary life. (Then again, you're looking for something extraordinary now.)

Read through the next section and really consider trying out the emotional release techniques. You can try them with a friend or two, with your partner, or alone. Some of you might feel better with a teacher, coach or other professional when you give it a try. Keep an open mind; sometimes during emotional release, the stuff that comes up will blow your mind. That's sort of the point.

A)   To do emotional release in the bona fide Tantric way, first get yourself some music with a primitive drum beat to it. It should have no words, just rhythm and music, preferably third world music. (You can order my CD, *Shamanic Release and Latihan*, for this express purpose.) Wear loose, comfortable clothing. Emotional release is very physical. Doing this clearing even once will make an astonishing difference to your emotional life. Doing it often will keep you clear and present. So why not do it?

B) Once you get the music going, lie down on the floor on your back with your knees bent so that your feet are flat on the floor. Put some pillows under your arms, down along your sides next to your hips. (You're going to be banging your arms down once you get going, and this is a precaution to prevent you from bruising.) Start with the arms up on the floor over your head. Listen to the music. It doesn't matter if you close your eyes or leave them open. You're going to start doing the Tantric *breathe and squeeze*.

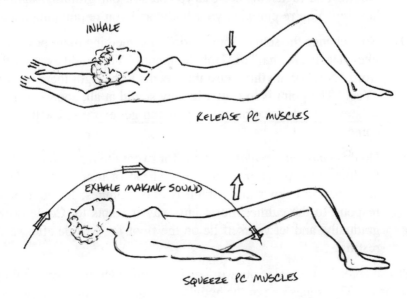

INHALE

RELEASE PC MUSCLES

EXHALE MAKING SOUND

SQUEEZE PC MUSCLES

Diagram 1

Begin squeezing your pelvic and rectal muscles rhythmically. Just do this a few times until you get a nice and steady beat going, not too fast. Once you have the rhythm, coordinate your exhale with the squeezing. Every time you squeeze the butt and sex muscles exhale with the sound "choo" again. You remember, we did this earlier in the chapter. It's exactly the same, only this time instead of sitting straight up, you're lying down.

You may notice that, as you squeeze, your pelvis rocks or tips up slightly like a sex thrust. And over time, you'll notice that your chin does it too, at the same time. I don't want to confuse you with too much here, but if your body starts thrusting up on the squeeze/exhale, this is good.

C) Now begin pumping the arms. As you squeeze/exhale making sound, slam your forearms down. As you breathe in, lift your forearms up over your head again. Squeeze/exhale; arms come down to your sides. Inhale; arms go up. Got it? You're not just placing your arms nicely on the floor when they come down, you're really pounding down. Again, you're not just breathing out of your mouth. You're making noise as you breathe out, grunting, sighing, heaving. You're pumping your body, and you're pumping hard.

D) Now change the sound from "choo" to something more powerful, like, "Ha, ha, ha, ha!" or "Huh, huh, huh!" You could even try the word "No!" or anything else that seems to be right there, maybe "Yes!" The point is to start with any sound at all; sooner or later whatever needs to come out of you and get expressed will surely come out.

E) Do this *emotional release* process for twenty to forty minutes. To facilitate this, program your music ahead of time to slow down and become calmer after about twenty minutes; let your body respond to the calmer music any way it wants to. Come down gradually, and let yourself lie on the floor for a while afterwards resting.

Please note: It's normal in our world to be afraid of letting your emotions come up. This squashing of the body's messages is actually *not* normal for humans, but it's probably what you were taught your whole life. For that reason, it's important to *be your own witness* during the course of all this emotional cleansing and releasing. Take one of those very small steps back from yourself and observe your body doing the practice, lying on the floor and making sounds.

Also notice your fear or your anger, your reluctance, or whatever you're feeling, from this witness distance. Just breathe and watch yourself in the process from the place of the witness. Notice yourself releasing pain and suffering. If you're someone with a lot of anger who usually finds your anger overwhelming and fearsome, take heart. It may feel like there isn't an end to it, but there is.

Memories

One time when I was doing emotional release, I noticed I was yelling, "No!" I yelled it over and over again with nothing important surfacing. That was just the word in my mouth at the time. Then, all of a sudden, an image of me as a little baby in a crib came before me and I started yelling at my parents, "Don't leave me alone yet. I'm too little. I need you. I'm afraid!!!!!!!!"

The more I said, "Don't leave me alone," the more I cried and screamed, just as I must have when I was an infant. At some point during the session, someone else who was in the room doing his own clearing reached over and held my hand. I cried quietly for a good long time and then at last it was over. When I say over, I mean over. I never had to revisit what had come up. It came up, went out, and I was done with it.

Some people have visions when they do Tantric *Emotional Release*. Other people realize that events that seemed to be innocuous in conscious memory are actually traumatic to the psyche. Some people can uncover memories of incest and abuse they had completely suppressed. Some yell and scream and sob and feel like they've been through the whole up and down of an immense emotional orgasm. Others don't.

However you experience it is how you experience it. Just keep witnessing the waves of whatever comes up. Witness the clearing and release, and then witness anything you discover about it, like any insights or newly found puzzle pieces to the mystery of you. Remember, there is no right or wrong here. It's all in the unknown, releasing pain and making room for pleasure. As in the body, so in the rest of life.

By the way, I had done a lot of transformational work myself by the time I found Tantra, but *being my own witness* during *emotional release* sessions moved me through a lifetime of hurt and anger that I thought was an integral part of me, the way my hair and skin and kidneys are a part of me. I promise that it will do the same for you.

Bill wrote in his poetic way: Crying. Crying for joy, for direction, for release. Wrestling, touching, stroking, holding close. Walking and letting it all rise up into the trees and the clouds. Letting the vast overtake the hideous thoughts of a small self. Opening the heart as I walk with arms flying apart before me and breath filling me in front and on the sides and low and high and back. Those terrific breathing exercises we did. Yelling that I am worthy to the walls and the stars. Listening calmly as my partner expresses herself and her fears and her concerns, her verbal release of the transactions and intersections of her day. No judging; listening. No fixing; listening. No mind wandering; focused listening to her need and her release.

Dynamic Meditation

Another popular method of clearing emotions is called *Dynamic Meditation*. This form of release was made famous by Osho, the Tantric master who lived in Pune, India, where an ashram dedicated to his principles still thrives.

I highly recommend this form of meditation because it was developed specifically for the "Western mind", a mind that has difficulty calming down, emptying out the constant mind chatter that besieges us on a moment by moment basis. I have modified it a little for my classes and here's how to do it:

A. Put on pumping, fabulous drum beat music (10 minutes) and put on a blindfold.

B. Put your hands up under your armpits and pump your elbows down when you pump your pelvis forward, like doing that old dance *The Funky Chicken*. Exhale and squeeze the buttocks and PC muscles when the pelvis is forward. (Similar to *Breathe and Squeeze*, but this time only through the nose and don't make any sounds on the exhale.)

C. At the end of the ten minute track, stop doing this chicken dance and make big sounds out of your mouth. Let anything come up and out for another ten minutes. Sound moves blocked energy so let it rip.

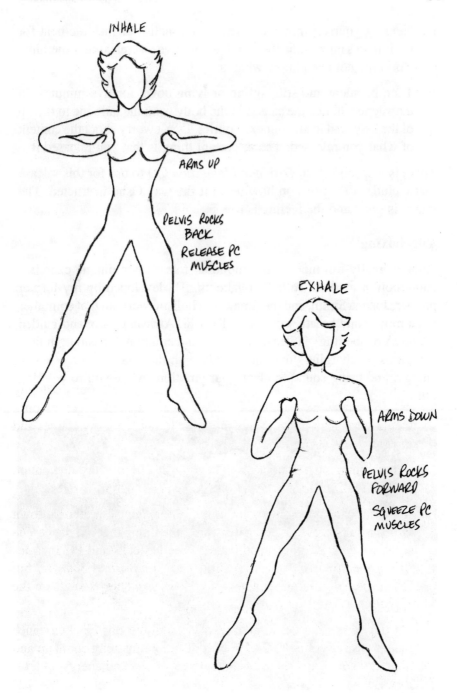

INHALE

ARMS UP

PELVIS ROCKS
BACK
RELEASE PC
MUSCLES

EXHALE

ARMS DOWN

PELVIS ROCKS
FORWARD

SQUEEZE PC
MUSCLES

Diagram 2

D. Next let yourself move and dance to a mellower melodic beat for ten minutes integrating the fact that you have just released something. You may not even know what!

E. Then be silent and still, sitting or lying down for five minutes. In the silence, notice the senses in the body from the tailbone to the tip of the head and in all your extremities. Don't worry about the content of what you released. The important thing is that you released it.

There is a special Osho *Dynamic Meditation* CD to use for this release that includes directions on how to do it the way Osho instructed. The music is great and the feeling is too.

Yogaboxing™

Another really fun method of emotional release is a unique exercise-and-emotion workout called Yogaboxing,™ developed by my former partner, Joshua Smith, and me. Imagine a holistic workout that combines yoga moves and breath work with Tai Chi, African dance, and guided chants. Yogaboxing™ releases physical and emotional tension. In fact, it focuses on charging your entire body with the vital life force/sexual energy, and using sound to clear your emotions while you're working out.

During the Yogaboxing™ workout, people do "boundary" work (I'll talk more about boundaries in a later chapter) and set intentions for themselves in the quiet, meditative period at the beginning of the workout. Then, while punching, they take turns yelling "No!" to what they don't want and "Yes!" to what they do want. Because of the music, the yelling and movement, people feel exhilarated and emotionally clear at the end of the workout, in much the same way they would feel clear at the end of the Tantric *Emotional Release* process.

You can order the *Original Yogaboxing* DVD from Butterfly Workshops. (See the back of book for recommended supplies and resources).

Be Here Now

One of the benefits of releasing this stuff is that you get to live right now, in the present, rather than reacting to issues from the past. Being present in the here and now makes it possible to be aware of and clear about what *you* want, and that's really important. I'll restate it, in case you missed the point: *Emotional Release* lets some of the emotional pressure drain away, so you can finally tune in to your own needs and feelings. When you live that way, aware of yourself, you'll see that you have more calm and less drama. Life naturally becomes more pleasurable. You don't have to force it. You'll be less frustrated and easier to please. By cleaning out the old junk, you make room for pleasure and bliss.

There's another great benefit to being clear. Having some kind of release for your emotions that does *not* involve your partner increases your trustworthiness within the relationship. It increases your tolerance for your partner's emotional responses as well, so you don't have to fall apart just because your lover has an emotional episode.

This newfound tolerance will open up deeper levels of intimacy in all your relationships. Your partner will see, very quickly, that it's okay to tell you things that weren't okay to tell you before. You'll be less reactive and less dangerous to the people you love. In other words, being emotionally clear will make you a better listener and a better friend. And thus a better lover, more capable of the kind of intimacy you are seeking through reading this book.

On that note, don't wait until you fall apart to do emotional clearing. Do it when you're upset, but also do it when you aren't. Just do it regularly. Do it as often as you fill up the gas tank. Do it more often than you change the oil. Just do it! I probably can't emphasize this enough, but let me try. Getting rid of the emotional garbage in your system, *not* by dumping it on someone else, but by releasing it through movement and sound, lets you function clean and clear with your beloved, yourself, and everyone you come into contact with. Clear out the gunk and run a clean emotional engine. You'll be so happy that you did, and so will all the people in your life. *Emotional Release* makes it possible for you actually to live in bliss and know it.

In the next chapter, we are going to deal with the most feared of all emotions in reference to intimacy, Anger. But first, let's recap what you've learned in this chapter, *Law III: Emotional Release*

- Feelings are natural; suppressing feelings is unnatural.

- Emotional pressure needs to be released like the steam in a pressure cooker: emotional release exercises help you blow off steam in a productive way so you can open to more intimacy.

- The Seven Chakras are the energy centers of the body.

- The two lower chakras, the root and sex chakras, are the keys to sexual energy.

- Tantric techniques help you move this vital energy throughout your body.

- Emotional Release Techniques help you remove toxins from the Chakras to allow for greater intimacy.

- There are a variety of Tantric Emotional Release Techniques: *Bioenergetic Release, Dynamic Meditation, Yogaboxing™*.

- Using Emotional Release Techniques on a regular basis will transform your relationships.

Law IV
Honor Your Anger

Anger is a signal, and one worth listening to.

– Harriet Lerner

Usually when people are sad, they don't do anything. They just cry over their condition. But when they get angry, they bring about a change.

– Malcolm X

The world needs anger. The world often continues to allow evil because it isn't angry enough.

– Bede Jarrett

I said in the previous chapter that I would write more about the energy of anger, and here we are, ready to deal with it. I think anger deserves its very own section in a book on sex and happiness because it is so misunderstood and yet so prevalent. With no permission for it to be expressed in healthy ways, repressed anger only contributes to the demise of intimacy – and society.

What, me angry?

To paint it broadly, people are angry, and not just "people", but *you*. You may be in denial about it, but unless you've done a tremendous amount of work processing your emotions, chances are you're angry as hell, and with good reason, too. How do I know? Listen, I'm a woman who has carried a lot of rage, so I feel like I have much to share about this particular emotion. And I'm not just talking about losing your temper because the car won't start. I'm talking about anger so intense and volatile that everyone is afraid of it.

And it's not just me. Take a look at the divorce statistics. Look at the rape, child abuse, and murder rates in America. Look at the number of people behind bars. What about the number of people on medication for their mood swings? Also, duh . . . our country is at war as I write this – and has been at war for years. Can you really afford to deny anger and make it wrong when you're so enveloped in it? To my way of thinking, it's time to acknowledge and deal with it, so we can do as much as we can to halt the damage it causes in our lives.

How to do that? Good question. My answer, the Tantric answer, is to embrace it. That's right, find the anger in yourself and embrace it with your whole heart. I know, this probably seems like a strange tactic, especially when society and all the major religions make anger so wrong. It's considered unholy, unspiritual, and downright unpleasant. How can you own and embrace this thing that's practically a sin? There's no place in an artificially sweetened culture for anger. How can you give yourself permission to own up to it, embrace it, and listen to its message?

Here's Osho's take on it:

Tantra says everything has to be absorbed, everything! Remember this, that Tantra accepts you in your totality. If you get a center of all your energies, you will be the richer if you have anger absorbed in it; you will be the richer if you have sex absorbed in it; you will be the richer if you have hatred, jealousy, absorbed in it – they are the spices of life, and you will taste...You will not become tasteless, you will have an enrichment to your taste. You need a little salt. And anger is exactly the same amount as is needed. When it overpowers you, it becomes ugly. If you eat only salt then you will die. Salt has a proportion, and in that proportion it is needed.

On the path, you will meet many people who would like to cripple you, to cut you, to dissect you. They will say, "This hand is bad, cut it off! This eye is bad, throw it out! Anger is bad, hate is bad, sex is bad." They will go to cutting you, and by the time they have left you, you are simply paralyzed, a crippled one. You have no life left. That's how the whole civilization has become paralyzed and crippled.

Osho – *Tantra the Supreme Understanding*

The Importance of Being Angry

I'm not advocating that you go out and bop the guy in the local café on the head for making your coffee wrong. I'm not advocating screaming at your partner because she looked at another man (unless that turns you both on). To *Honor your Anger* isn't the same thing as indulging your temper. Temper is what you have when you don't take your wants and needs seriously enough to get them met. Instead you revert back to childhood tantrums and hope that some adult will take care of these wants and needs for you. Acting out your temper is actually another way of being a victim. And depression? It's anger turned inward, anger turned on yourself. If you think you're not angry, but you know you're depressed, I've got news for you. You're angry. So listen up!

Anger is important. It's telling you something about yourself and about your life, about what isn't acceptable to you. When the anger rises (or the tears come), you don't have to act on it, but in order to evolve emotionally and spiritually you do have to listen. Anger is a fight reaction that comes straight from lizard brain's small but essential repertoire of responses – "fight," "flight," or "freeze."

Anger is a natural response to danger; it's deeply involved in your survival. Survival helps you outlast fear and threat. In other words, when you're angry, it's because you feel threatened and you want to survive. Something is threatening you. What is it? Discover that, and you have the key to working with your anger in a positive, not destructive way.

The Angry Woman

In Harriet Lerner's wonderful book, *The Dance of Anger*, she talks about women choosing early on in life whether they're going to be "the nice girl" or be "the bitch." It's a big decision. Most women don't want to be angry. Choose the bitch role and other women can turn on you. Choose the bitch role and figure on emasculating your husband. Or choose nice girl and choose victimhood.

Either way, it's a no-win situation. Lock yourself into either role and you get the same result: Nothing changes. As a nice girl you get to sacrifice yourself and end up depressed and miserable. As bitch you get to stomp other people into shivery fear and end up misunderstood and miserable anyway.

Tantra has a different view, symbolized by the goddess Kali:

> In Tantra we often refer to Kali, who is considered the forceful form of the great goddess. Kali is represented as a black

woman with three eyes, and four arms; in one hand she has a sword and in another the head of the demon she has slain, symbolizing slaying the demon of ignorance. With the other two she is encouraging her worshippers to "fear not." For earrings she has two dead bodies, and she wears a necklace of skulls; her only clothing is a girdle made of dead men's hands, and her tongue protrudes from her mouth. Her eyes are red, and her face and breasts are besmeared with blood. She stands with one foot on the thigh and another on the breast of her husband, Shiva. Upon first glance, she can be mistaken as being the Goddess of death, sex and violence, but this is an incorrect interpretation. She is the most misunderstood deity of all.

Kali means "time" in Sanskrit, because she devours time. Many people see a fearsome creature, but spiritually mature people see the compassionate mother. She is the annihilator of all and anything that is not worth keeping, and in doing so, she helps people recognize their truth in the spiritual sense.

Kali's blackness symbolizes her all-embracing, comprehensive nature because black is the color in which all other colors merge; black absorbs and dissolves them.

Kali's nudity has a similar meaning. In many instances she is described as garbed in space, or as being sky-clad. In her absolute, primordial nakedness she is free from all covering of illusion. She is Nature, stripped of clothes, symbolizing that she is completely beyond name and form. Her nudity is said to represent totally illumined consciousness, unaffected by maya (false consciousness). Kali is the bright fire of truth that cannot be hidden by the clothes of ignorance. Such truth simply burns them away.

Kali is full-breasted, her motherhood a ceaseless creation. Her wildly untamed hair forms a curtain of illusion, the fabric of space-time that organizes matter out of the chaotic sea of quantum-foam. Her hair is a symbol of her stormy nature, as well as her femininity. Her garland of fifty human heads, each representing one of the fifty letters of the Sanskrit alphabet, symbolizes the repository of knowledge and

The Goddess Kali

wisdom. She wears a girdle of severed human hands, hands that are the principle instruments of work and thus signify the action of karma (cause and effect). The binding effects of this karma have been overcome, severed as it were, by devotion to Kali. She has blessed the devotee by cutting him free from the cycle of karma.

Her white teeth are symbolic of purity, and her lolling red tongue dramatically illustrates that she consumes all things and denotes the act of tasting or enjoying what society regards as forbidden, i.e., her indiscriminate enjoyment of all the world's "flavors."

Kali's four arms represent the complete circle of creation and destruction, which is contained within her. She represents the inherent creative and destructive rhythms of the cosmos. Her right hands making the mudras of "fear not," represent the creative aspect of Kali, while the left hands, holding a bloodied sword and a severed head, represent her destructive aspect. The bloodied sword and severed head symbolize the destruction of ignorance and the dawning of knowledge. The sword is the sword of knowledge that cuts the knots of ignorance and destroys false consciousness (the severed head). Kali opens the gates of freedom with this sword, having cut the eight bonds that bind human beings.

Finally, her three eyes represent the sun, moon, and fire with which she is able to observe the three modes of time: past, present and future. This attribute is also the origin of the name Kali, which is the feminine form of "Kala," the Sanskrit term for Time.

– Excerpted from www.Wikipedia.com and Rosa Santana in *Enlightened Practice Magazine* March/April 2005

Some women are ruled by Kali, and some women are afraid of the Kali power in them and refuse to claim it. You cut through the bullshit of life and relationships, but not always in the most constructive ways. Many of you women would never declare war in a direct manner, but you certainly have been known to withhold sex to wield the power in your relationship, or use it as a bargaining chip to "win" with your partner. But without true intimacy, no one wins.

And can you women nag or what? You bring up the same old incident over and over again, even though it took place five years ago and is supposed to be over and done with. But you don't know the meaning of over and done with. When it seems strategically convenient, you pull it right out again as if it has been waiting to be dusted off and used as the weapon it is. Now, how would I know this? Humm? Listen, I've tried this many times myself and seen no positive results. Anger used as a destructive weapon in a relationship severs the relationship. Passive aggression, a covert expression of anger does the same. In Tantra, we find methods for releasing the Kali in us, and regain our deepest sense of power and selfhood in the process.

In my Ecstasy workshop, during the *puja* (an honoring ritual for goddesses and gods), I created a part where women get to play the Goddess Kali. Many of them just cannot allow themselves to do it. They cannot be that direct with the playful power of destruction even though they all have Kali power in them. When they do let themselves play it out fully and honestly, they have so much fun, and so do the men who receive it as a gift from the goddess.

The Angry Man

Of course, men are angry too, and that anger is often very scary. Men have become afraid of their own anger, and it certainly terrifies women. Even now in our supposedly more enlightened Western society, masculine anger terrifies women into a certain kind of carefulness or craftiness that men consider dishonest and women consider essential to their survival. When men are filled with such anger, and so unable to find an acceptable outlet for it, it's almost a relief when the testosterone drops at forty. Okay, so the love handles come and the nice hair goes, but at least the fury goes away with it. Or *seems* to. Even tamped down as passive aggression, this anger has a destructive force of its very own which erodes and eventually destroys intimacy. Rather than a cataclysmic "breaking up," this kind of anger produces the strangulation of passion and slow suffocation of a relationship.

As I see it, one big problem in our society is that men aren't taught to be *men* anymore. There is no process for boys to be initiated into the world of adult males as there is in traditional societies. That means a lot of uninitiated boys are walking around in men's bodies attempting to have masculine power, and relationships with women. The only place men have permission to be men and show aggression is in sporting activities like football, where only a few are able to play, but all the other men get to yell, "Kill them!" at the other team. By the way, erectile dysfunction is at an all-time high, with numerous drugs to treat it. Just how "manly" is the Cialis Invitational Golf Tournament or Levitra Formula One Racing? Or just sitting around watching them on TV?

Many men I know have shared that their most powerful edge, their most passionate time, was on the front lines in war. Could that be re-occurring now? Have we created war so that men can get their testosterone up again?

Thousands of years of power, strength and aggression – the very essence of maleness – have diminished in a matter of a "sensitive" decade or three. Unfortunately, many of these sensitive men are losing their ability to get it up, losing their power, their *potency*. That's right. Many men come to me for Tantra because they think they need Viagra. Viagra shmiagra!!! All they need is to grant themselves permission to feel their male aggression soaring through their veins again. Get some of that testosterone flowing, and they can be as virile as ever. Really, the challenge is what to do with the anger each and every one of us possesses. Declaring war is not necessarily the answer. Moving and channeling their latent sexual energy, as we discussed in Law III: *Emotional Release*, is the answer.

Beating Up the Car

Let me tell you a story. I had a client, a woman, who took my workshops and then referred her husband to me for some private sessions. She was afraid of him. Nothing bad had ever happened, but she was scared. She knew that underneath his perfect control lurked a monster of rage, and she worried about what would happen when that monster finally reared its head.

So I met with him and saw how anger was shaking in him just beneath the surface. I sent him home with an assignment. The assignment was to find a big rubber mallet. Every day after work, before he even entered the house, he had to spend twenty to thirty minutes beating the hell out of an old junker car he had in the backyard with that heavy mallet, just beating on it until he was sweating and tired and clear, an extreme form of *Emotional Release,* but in his case, an extremely successful one.

That's right. This practice saved their relationship. He now had a safe outlet for his rage. Each time he emptied out his anger, he felt safe enough to express all his other emotions. Then he and his wife entered into the deeply intimate love affair they had both always wanted and had been unable to access previously.

Most men, and quite a few women, need something like a rubber mallet and an old car. They need a safe outlet for their anger. Later on they can process at will, but until their anger is honored and provided for, it will control them from under the surface and dominate their lives. And damage all their relationships as a result.

In and Out of Anger

I've had friends who medicated themselves for years in order to try to deal with their scary anger. I've had other friends whose families wished like hell they had medicated themselves. There are people whose lesson is in finding and claiming their own anger, and some of them will draw rage-aholics to them like bees to honey. That way there's always someone else being angry, and they never have to go there themselves.

Personally I notice that I can flip-flop, either drawing anger from people or dealing it out myself. My primary self-expression, though, used to be howling fury, and I was always the angry one. Since I've spent a few years doing Tantra and *Emotional Release*, I find all that rage has ... transformed. Before, my anger was so all-encompassing that I never felt like I had a choice in the matter. I just exploded, and then, after the explosion, dealt with the damage. After learning about Tantra and doing a lot of *Emotional Release* work, I eventually got the concept of embracing my anger fully, rather than trying (and always failing) to squash it down. Interestingly, once I brought that shadowy, dark, shameful part of myself into the light, the force of it seemed to diminish on its own. Now it's not such a big deal to take responsibility for my anger and clear it out *before* the next incident happens. I just don't have that much stored up inside me any more. In my life that's a miracle!

My experience with going deep into anger is that when I go all the way through it to the other side, I am filled with tears of joy and compassfon for myself, which then flows out to others. That's why I said in the previous chapter that there's an end to the seething pit of anger, even when you think there isn't. There really is. But you have first to honor where you are now, what you're going through. Shame and suppression will only keep things exactly as they are – stopped, blocked, stuck.

How It's Done

The first step to *Honor Your Anger* is simply to witness it without judgment and without taking action. In a quiet moment, when you aren't angry or afraid, take a good look at anger and how it figures in your life. Do you give in to it when it arises, or do you suppress it? Do you have shame about it, or regrets about how you handle it? Just notice these things. Try to notice and, of course, do some emotional clearing. Find a safe jungle room where you can do some roaring and roaming and release until you're feeling human again.

Then, when you're able to focus, concentrate on what would please you, and I mean in the deepest, most gratifying way. What would feed your bliss? What would contribute to your happiness, and can you get some of it into your life, like right now?

You might need to experiment with allowing yourself to get angry when you are not necessarily angry at anyone or with anything in the current moment. Basically you're going to get on the floor and do emotional release. Use your hands to beat down on the pillows beside you and whack away just as I described in the last chapter. When you've gotten to the point of hitting really hard and getting lost in it, then yes, start yelling.

Allow yourself to express any of the unreasonable things you feel like saying, but usually censor because you judge them as unfair, unreasonable, unladylike, ungentlemanly, out of character, embarrassing, etc. Say things like, "I hate you! I hate you!" or "How dare you! How dare you!"

Repeat the sentence over and over again, beginning softly and then getting progressively louder and louder. If anyone you know comes to mind as you do this, add their name to the sentence, and experience what it feels like to say, "I hate you, (dad, mom, boss, friend, neighbor, whomever)!" "I'm so angry at you!" "You really hurt me!" Give yourself permission to yell freely. Please don't worry here about whether it seems logical, fair or politically correct.

At first, you may not totally feel these things. You may not ever want to say them to another person (and I don't advise that you do), but if the feelings exist in you and go unexpressed, they will fester. Of this I am sure. This so-called "unacceptable" emotion gets in the way of your enjoying your alone time and your time with your partner. It takes so much effort to hold onto and resist the unacceptable, repressed feelings that they end up blocking your vital energy, and thus blocking any genuine intimacy. Once you let the anger and other repressed feelings out, during a release session, you will be freer to put your attention and energy into the present in the rest of your life.

Often resentment from repressed anger comes out as sexual coldness or verbal abuse, and is a weapon used by both genders which destroys any hope of intimacy. The next time your partner approaches you sexually and you notice that you feel distant or annoyed, ask yourself, "What am I angry and resentful about? Am I holding out now because I failed to express myself fully before? Do I even know why I am angry?" Just witness.

Then, after doing *Emotional Release*, go ahead take the next big step toward true Tantric intimacy, and share your feelings with your partner. It might be embarrassing or potentially hurtful, but chronically rejecting your lover is more hurtful, and opens up a wider and wider chasm between you. One that may never be crossed. If you've practiced saying unforgivable things while screaming out your anger and upset to the sound of primitive music in your *Emotional Release* sessions, then the act of expressing your feelings calmly to another person, instead of choosing a weapon to protect yourself, will come more easily. With practice you'll be much more in tune with all your feelings and emotions; you will learn to speak up *before* you're blind with anger. You and the other people in your life will all find relief in this, great relief.

Using "I" statements is key when you finally do express the feelings to your partner minus the emotional charge. Examples of "I" statements are, "I resent you for_____," "I am angry at you for_____," "I was hurt and upset when _____." "I haven't felt safe around you since _____."

While expressing the anger or other strong feelings, you may need to drop into the body and describe the exact sensations you are having at the very moment of communication. It involves your witnessing what the body is telling you and then saying that to the other person. For example, "I notice I feel tight in the chest and a bit nauseous in the belly. My palms feel sweaty. Oh, I feel afraid to tell you how angry I am with you. And I am angry with you."

Using "I" statements helps you to remember that the focus here is you, not your partner. It's not your job to diagnose your partner, to accuse your partner, or to pretend you know what's "really" going on with your partner. Try to be more respectful than that, especially you women (oh no, more inflaming!), who like to think you can "figure out" what's going on for your occasionally silent partners.

Nobody likes to be diagnosed and accused, so even if you're mad and righteous, just keep breathing and witnessing and focus on naming *your* feelings and reactions. When you use the word "I" and then describe what *you* feel, you'll find a way to open up conversation that can solve a problem. Using "you" statements will only shut your partner down, turn you into an accuser, and lock you both into old accusing patterns that are barriers to intimate knowing of each other's inner truths.

Learning to Ask

I have found it invaluable to use "I" statements when expressing difficult emotions to another person, but that alone isn't always enough. It helps to know what you want or expect from the other, because after sharing what you're feeling – and actually hearing the response – it will probably be necessary to make a request.

You might request that the person stop a certain behavior, like telling jokes about you. Or you might have to request an apology. That's right, sometimes people do not readily apologize, but you've probably already noticed this. So, if an apology is what you want, go ahead and ask for it.

When you receive it, pause for a moment to accept the apology into your body, and notice if that helps how you're feeling. If it doesn't help, you might need to make another request. For example, "Thank you for saying you're sorry. I realize, though, that I need you to look directly at me, so I can feel connected to you when you say it. Please look into my eyes and say again what you just said."

Sometimes You Feel Like a Nut

It takes courage to ask for what you need. Here's something to keep in mind, however. You can't control the other person. You're only in charge of *you*, after all. So sometimes when you ask people for something, they can honor your request; sometimes they can't. They might not be ready, or it might not fit in with their life's purpose or their integrity. How can they be happy being forced to promise you something that would alter or interfere with their own life? After you share your feelings and listen to the response, ask for what you want, and then listen to the answer. You may or may not get exactly what you want. After sharing like this, however, you will definitely have a new place emotionally to move into together.

Mind you, it still comes down to what you will do with your anger, if any, over being "slighted." At best, you can request an apology from the other person, knowing that they really don't want you to hurt and did what they did accidentally. The people in your life don't know that something will affect you the way it does. You don't know how you're going to affect them, either. It's an honoring and also a knowing that someone can't make a promise about *it never happening again*. Realistically, it's not possible for someone else to know all of your triggers. You probably don't know them yourself, not until you're freaking out and armoring up, and reptile brain is already on code red.

So Whose Fault is This?

All of this raises some interesting questions about where the responsibility lies for the feelings in the first place. I've learned to be responsible for the anger I feel. I don't know where it came from and I don't know why it has been such a strong force in my life, but by doing both *Emotional Release* and communicating straight – *Speaking My Truth* – when I am angry or upset, the burden has lifted. Looking back, I can see that the anger resided deep in me, and was scary to my loved ones and to me as well. I also see that an incident only triggered anger in me because the anger was there to begin with. Go figure.

It's not a question of whether to have anger or not, or even whether anger is good or bad. Anger is neither. It just *is*. And, by the way, it cannot really be removed anyway, as in cut out or thrown away in the garbage. So the question of what to do with it remains. Something has to be done, but what?

I finally realized (or chose to assume) that the people in my life don't purposely want to hurt me or anger me by their actions toward me. True, I might get hurt or angry, but that has more to do with what's inside me, my expectations, than with what their motivations are. Practicing *Emotional Release* gets rid of the anger inside me, so I don't get triggered much anymore. But it still happens, and I still have to share my feelings and make my requests. I inadvertently anger other people too, and they have to make their requests of me. That's human nature, making those "mistakes." It's how you learn about each other, and it's how you grow. I'll go so far as to say it's part of the beauty of being with someone else. I see it as a vital part of the intimate dance between women and men learning the path to eternal ecstasy.

What I know for sure is that in honoring my own anger rather than making myself wrong for having it in the first place, I have been able to work with it, express it, and release it. I've come to more peace than I dreamed possible. What I think has happened is that I've come through to the other side. On this new side, mostly I feel filled with compassion. *Honoring My Anger* has allowed me to do this.

I know you, too, can come to this peace for yourself. You may not come away with the answers to all life's questions, but you will feel a whole lot better. I can tell you that after all the work I've done; I still have so many questions about life. Oh well. I guess we'll be in on the quest together. Let's go!

Law V: Speak Your Truth is the next law of Tantric Intimacy we'll be covering to help us in our quest for more blissful relationships. But before we move on, let's have another look at what we've covered in *Law IV: Honor Your Anger*.

In this chapter, you've learned:

- People deny that they are angry because socially and spiritually they are encouraged to suppress it.

- Anger is important in the process of transformation when honored and expressed in healthy ways.

- Anger can be a great barrier to intimacy when it is expressed as physical or verbal abuse.

- Men and women need regular emotional clearing in order to be emotionally available to one another in true intimacy.

- Men and women need to learn how to express their anger straight and ask for what they need.

- You need to own and take responsibility for your anger.

Law V
Speak Your Truth

Even the fear of death is nothing compared to the fear of not having lived authentically and fully. I've grown certain that the root of all fear is that we've been forced to deny who we are.

— Frances Moore Lappe

You tell the truth about your judgments and opinions and experiences. You are explicit about what you have done, what you think and what you feel. You hang in there. You fall in love again. True intimacy is based on sharing honestly the way your life is for you, what you think and what you feel — and let the chips fall where they may.

— Brad Blanton

The truth will set you free, but first it will piss you off!

— Werner Erhart

Most people don't tell the truth. I'm not even referring to telling the truth about sex, although that's certainly the case. If you were honest, you'd admit that you aren't honest, not about the movies you like, the friends you prefer, or how you want to spend your time. You pretend to like things that you don't, act as if you're shocked by things you don't give a damn about, and most of all, you cover up your real hurts so no one knows how vulnerable you are.

You Are the Great Pretender

If you're like most people, you've pretended your way through the bulk of your life, misguidedly thinking it was the way to more gold stars and a higher rung on the ladder. Early on you learned to decipher the clues about what society expects you to think and feel, and then you set about trying to think and feel that way. You've spent decades suppressing your true self and now you're beginning to realize it. Now you're rediscovering yourself under all that protective, pretentious crap. Do you know where the discovery is leading you? Straight to love and romance, my friends.

First there's the romance with yourself you haven't experienced since childhood (and that's if you were lucky). Second, if you're really, really lucky, you'll be able to create mind-blowing, truly rewarding intimacy with another human being. You might be ready. Or you might wonder how to have a romance at all when the simple act of connection – genuine human connection – seems absolutely beyond reach.

Wherever you are on the dating/mating spectrum, there's one little problem in the way of any relationship. As soon as you hook up with another human being and attempt anything intimate, the first thing you both do is pretend to be someone else entirely. Why? For fear the new person just might walk away if they knew who you *really* were. The irony being, of course, that all of us want to be loved for our true self!

Four-and-Twenty Lies a Day

Speaking Your Truth means being authentic about who you are and what you want, and to hell with public and private opinion about what's termed "appropriate". By the time you've gotten to this point in your life, though, you've already spent a long time covering up who you are. You may not notice how skillfully you side-step your genuine thoughts and reactions. Your real feelings are still there, but you acknowledge them only to ask if they would please shut up and stop making trouble.

Here's a rough estimate of the daily lying quota: There's social lying that's become second nature, especially at work. There are those little white relationship lies that have become so much easier to tell than the pain-causing truth. There are things you tell yourself about your life that you used to know weren't true but have sort of forgotten. There are the lies you tell your kids to get them to behave and turn out successfully, and the lies you tell other parents so you'll look like a good mom or dad.

You lie to your doctor about your habits, lie to the insurance company about where you drive your car and lie to your partners about sex. You lie about your hunger and your hurts. When someone asks if you're feeling OK, without thinking you lie and say yes. Most of the time it doesn't cross your mind to tell the truth. When it comes down to brass tacks to see what in your life is worth being brutally honest about, the answer is not a lot.

The reason you're reading a book on intimacy, and I'm leading workshops on intimacy and sex and happiness, is that by the time you've learned to make it in society, you've become seriously out of touch with yourself. How in hell are you supposed to know and love another person when you don't even know and love yourself? Those years of second-guessing and disguising your actual opinions have led you, inevitably, into not knowing the first thing about what you actually think and feel anymore. If you don't know what you think and feel, how can you expect to be at the state you want in terms of speaking your truth?

Personal Integrity

People are addicted to looking good, which is another big obstacle to intimacy. You have to get over the traumas of high school in order to grow up and be worthy of a vibrant and authentic relationship. You have to put aside your need for public approval and your fear of looking ridiculous in order to own and express your honest response. That is a big deal. For example, I know there are many of you who, trying to be all things to all people, say, "Yes", when you mean, "No", to invitations and requests from the people in your life.

The way I stopped myself from doing that very thing was that if someone called to invite me to an event, or to ask me to do something for them – and after I hung up the phone I realized I had said yes to something I really didn't want to do – I would immediately call back.

(As an aside, though, I have to stop for a moment to talk about integrity and keeping my word. I have it that when I give my word to something, I keep it. I regard my word as my personal law. So what was I to do with an invitation or request I had just accepted that I knew was out of alignment with my desires, my dreams, and the option to use my time as I wish? For me this has been a big lesson in personal integrity.)

As I was saying, as soon as I realized I had agreed to something I didn't want to do, I would immediately call back. When the person answered I would say something like, "You know, at the risk of our relationship, I need to tell you that I just lied to you. I told you I wanted to do this thing with/for you, but I knew as soon as I hung up that it was not my truth."

"One of the things I'm growing into is being authentic and only making commitments to those things to which I am truly committed. I am not committed to this. I am committed to our relationship, however, so I apologize for steering you wrongly. I'm sorry if this has caused you hurt or inconvenience. I'm telling you as quickly as possible so you're not spending a lot of time counting on me when you can use this time as an opportunity to invite (or make a request of) someone else."

Do you know that nine times out of ten this has turned out to be an amazingly freeing gesture for me and for the recipient? I've been able to stay in integrity with myself, following my inner guidance, *and* stay in integrity with others. Over time, it has increased my self-love and has increased my love for and from others.

Unlovable Me

A primary force in your relationships is how afraid you are of rejection. You run around in circles like a panicked hamster: "I've got to do this or I won't be loved!" and "I've got to do that or I won't be loved!" You've never taken the time to find out what you really want, what your partner really wants, and hey, can you do some negotiating while you're doing the dishes?

Given that you have this need for looking good and pleasing people, what if you end up looking like a fool and then get rejected as well? Or what if you end up actually making your beloved mad at you, so mad that she yells and screams and won't have sex with you anytime in the foreseeable future? What if your man gets so furious and hurt he doesn't speak to you for a week or actually scares you with his anger? What if your sweetheart cries and sobs and can't believe you really and truly feel like that about anything? Oh, the horror. Oh, the drama. Please don't think it's enough to make you never speak up at all. It isn't. It's far worse in the long run to suppress yourself, than to just face up to the truth.

Speaking Your Truth, even at the risk of being left by (or wanting to leave) your partner, is mandatory for a successful intimate relationship. There's *no* way around it. Most people who know me would certainly say that I speak my truth. Yet I too catch myself holding back. One of the ways I caught myself not being authentic was by not saying everything I wanted at any given time. For example, if my partner was going to the grocery store, I only gave him a partial list for fear I would be asking too much.

Think for a minute how this translated into sex. I would stop myself from speaking up and saying exactly what I wanted, what my particular tastes were, and what would really turn me on, for fear I'd be asking too much. Or, worse, for fear of being judged for liking sex too much. Or being "bad" for desiring a particular thing. So what was my partner supposed to do, become a mind reader?

Public Speaking 101

I can hear a lot of people gasping (or dropping to the floor in a faint) at the prospect of having to speak up. You probably don't like that idea too well, unless there's a guarantee of a good listener out there to receive your words kindly. Well, here's the bad news: as often as not, there's some pretty lousy listening out there, and that's from both sexes.

Men, you don't listen by doing the adult equivalent of putting your hands over your ears and saying, "I can't hear you, I can't hear you." You let your woman know in some subtle and some crude ways that what she says is not important. Maybe you read the newspaper while she's talking to you, or turn on the TV sports channel but keep on insisting that you can hear what she's saying.

Women, you think you listen, but you really don't. You feign listening, in reality listening selectively, and then you have a total conniption fit when your man says something you don't approve of. You think a man can talk easily into that kind of space? Ha.

I had a student in Boston a long time ago whose husband used to read the paper whenever she talked to him. She wanted him to put the paper down and pay full attention to her when she spoke about things important to her. He just refused to put that paper down, insisting he could listen while reading. One day they were scheduled to go somewhere and she offered to drive. When they were both in the car and had taken to the road, she hopped onto the Massachusetts Turnpike. He questioned her as to where she was going since it was not necessary to take the Pike to go where they were headed. She said, "I want you to listen to me with your undivided attention and I am prepared to drive straight to the end of the Mass Pike until we finish this subject completely. I want a real conversation. Got that?"

Well evidently, her husband sat straight up in the passenger seat and they had a regular repartee about the subject that was really important to her. The way the story goes, they only had to go as far as Framingham (a half hour outside Boston) before she was satisfied and they turned back. I like this example because nobody got hurt. They probably laughed at what it took to just communicate.

Now you don't have to go that far necessarily. Or maybe you do! But having an ideal audience is really not the objective anyway. The objective is not how your words are received. I mean, sure, it's nice when your partner can be all evolved and receptive and really listen, and then really get what you're saying and then really support you in what you want without being hurt or impatient or reptile-brain activated. But frankly, that's a pipe dream. Or anyway it only happens sometimes. And has a lot to do with your expectations of what you want to happen in this situation. You can't wait for it all to be perfect. You can't afford to. That's letting someone else decide whether or not you're worthy enough to speak up in this lifetime, and it's not up to someone else to decide that. Only you can. Sorry, Charlie, but you have to make that judgment call yourself, and have the guts to speak your truth.

The reason you need to speak your truth in an intimate relationship, even at the risk of romantic rejection, is because it's crucial for *you*. There's no such thing as mind-blowing intimacy, passion and love built on pretense and fear. You, innocent you, are also reptile-brain activated when your friends and lovers speak their truth. Their reactions might scare you into silence, but you can take it to the bank that your reactions scare them into silence, too. The truth has to start somewhere. You're reading this book. Let the truth start with *you*.

Risks and Consequences

By the way, by truth I don't mean truthful nagging, and I don't mean truthful raging. You can be gentle and truthful just as easily as you can be harsh and truthful. Well, maybe not just as easily. It may take some figuring at first. Better to be harsh and truthful – and clean up after yourself – then sweep the truth under the rug again for the sake of deceptive harmony, which is really little or no "relating" in a relationship at all.

Once you practice *Emotional Release* on an ongoing basis, and also practice speaking your truth, it's only natural that you become gentler, more tolerant, and more compassionate, toward yourself as well as your partner/s. It will become easier, over time.

You should know, however, that each new move toward openness and connection with another person is accompanied by fear. Revealing yourself involves huge risk. If you can embrace your fear each time you feel yourself shedding a layer, then you can ultimately open more deeply to yourself and your partner/s and achieve a richer intimacy. At first, though, you'll probably just be scared to death. Be ready for it and *Speak Your Truth* anyway. You can always say, "I'm afraid to tell you this and I'm going to say it anyway." Then proceed.

Usually it looks like this: You'll want to risk some huge revelation. While you're sweating over it and whether your sweetheart can handle it, you'll suddenly come up with reasons to break up, or you'll get drunk for a week, or maybe you'll start an enormous fight. You might even turn on yourself and get depressed. Any or all of these reactions crop up because you want to change a powerful, long-term thing about yourself. You want to set aside a demon that's had you in its grip, and the demon doesn't want to go.

Revealing yourself is plain scary, and it takes courage and wisdom to see it through. A sense of humor doesn't hurt. Sure, you want change. You also want nothing to change. That's just your human nature and your reptile brain, dancing together down the yellow brick road. What are you going to do about it?

Bernice said, "My relationship just keeps moving forward, although it didn't seem so promising in the beginning. He loves that I speak my truth to him; it increases our intimacy. I get such great responses from him now because as my self-esteem goes up, his self-esteem goes up as well."

Can You See Me Now?

All people yearn to be truly seen and loved for who they are. You, your lover, your children, even your parents want to be truly *seen*, and that way be known and loved. You may have noticed, however, that you don't make this too easy on other people, and they don't make it easy on you. In fact, you pretty much play hide and seek with your true self and force the people in your life to search for the real you over and over again. Maybe they do it successfully, maybe they don't. The point is that you hide your true self away through some type of lying on a daily basis which I mentioned at the start of this chapter. Of course you do it because you think you have to in order to be accepted, or because you've been hurt, but hiding your true self away doesn't take care of the hurt. It only leaves you feeling rejected and unloved, and sometimes resentful and angry to boot.

I can just hear some of you saying, "But wait, it's not my fault! I'm not the one who said my true self should hide away forever. I didn't want to hide. It was society and my parents and my first few lovers who let me know how unacceptable I was, not me. Now you're blaming me for responding to criticism by protecting myself!"

I know, I know, it's that way for all of us on this long road to adulthood, and I'm not blaming you for anything. Your behavior is a perfectly sane and understandable way of handling all those painful, learning-how-to deal-with-society, growing-up pressures. It's just that now you're here in whatever year of your life, of adulthood, and I assume you want to truly enjoy yourself. Now you're here at relationship or marriage number whatever (who can keep track anymore?) trying to achieve genuine intimacy and magical sex. You've been there, done that, sent the postcard. But bliss isn't outside yourself – the place you have to start is inside you. In Tantra you have to start by really seeing yourself, and honoring what you see, all of it, no matter what you find. That's how *Speaking your Truth* begins. You first have to see what your truth is. Then you have to muster your courage and spit it out.

Speak, Breathe, Speak

I have to tell you something, though. It's not your partner's job to make this easy for you. You can blame your lover for your silence, your eggshell-walking, your temper tantrums, your over-eating and your screwing around for exactly as long as you want to stay untransformed. If you're ready to wake up and bring joy and intimacy into your life now, right now, with whatever kind of monster or icicle or angel or prince you happen to be hooked up with, then start telling the truth about yourself.

Start with low risk things that you may have been hiding, like your food preferences, your interests, and things you honestly do not care for. Next share the middle risk things like how you feel about swearing or about people being late. Build up to high risk things like what you really want for your birthday, or what wild sex thing you want her or him to perform on you in bed.

Important Note: It's not your job to control how your partner reacts. You can't do that in this lifetime, okay, so stop trying already. It'll just drive you both crazy. I mean really, do you like it when your friends and family try to control your feelings and reactions? No, and you didn't like it as a child, either. Nobody likes it, certainly not your spouse. It's not your job, and it's not your business. Your job is to manage *you*, and believe me, that's plenty.

Love in the Dark

People (not just me and you) are under the misguided notion that their true and actual self is an undesirable, hideous thing. I don't know where this notion comes from exactly, but it's universal. You did some complicated 2+2=5 thing as a kid and decided that, because you got in trouble for this infraction or that bad report card, people were disgusted by you and you'd better hide your disgusting true self or never be loved again.

In one of my courses, people have to share their skeletons, as in "skeletons in the closet". It's been really an eye-opening process for people because they find out that everyone around them generally knows the skeleton they've been hiding. In some cases where the skeleton was well-hidden, it turns out that people love them more for their humanity once the skeleton is out. Usually, the person who has been hiding their particular skeleton sighs with relief after the secret is out, and their whole life shifts into greater ease. It's the process of disclosing that frees you up to be authentically who you are.

Intimacy in the Tantric sense – mind-blowing intimacy and the love that follows – is about exposing the depths of your soul and going into the depths of human experience. There is nothing superficial about

Tantra. It isn't about having a "nice" relationship as much as it is about having a "real" relationship.

My advice is to go ahead and unleash that dark self as soon as you can. Bring it into the light and own its power. It's going to howl and prowl and haunt you until you do anyway, and guess what? You won't be one iota less lovable than you are now. In fact, it's the only way to let love in. Love has to reach your dark, deep self, or it doesn't feel real, so give your darkness some words. *Speak your truth.* Own your truth. Breathe and witness and feel your truth. And by knowing and loving your authentic self, others can too.

Back and Back to the Body Beautiful

Here's how to speak your truth: Let the sensations and emotions in your body guide you. Take anger for example. When your reptile brain rears up its ferocious killer head, you're onto something. Maybe your partner has just squashed you in the same way your parents used to. Maybe your lover just did something you were *never* allowed to do, something that you were taught was wrong, wrong, wrong, and here it is right in your face. Ooh, reptile brain hates that. When reptile brain gets activated with anger, something important – a clue to your psyche – is showing itself for decoding.

By the way, anger for some people is carefully and seemingly safely turned inward. They stopped feeling their own anger long ago. If that's the case for you, let depression be your guide. If you're crying over the laundry and bad weather and basically everything else in your life, go and do some deep emotional clearing. Then take yourself gently by the hand, take a deep breath, and start, please, please, please, start to *speak your truth.* The problem is that your inner self is dying from neglect. That's what those tears and ingrown anger are all about.

By the way Tantric work is not meant to replace psychotherapy or counseling. If you feel depressed, you may want to seek professional help. At a minimum, counseling is as good a place as any where you can practice speaking your truth instead of suppressing it.

It's all right to start small with this stuff because the ripples spread. Whatever it is, whenever you see yourself do that little squash-down, nobody-wants-to-hear-this-anyway evasive maneuver, STOP. Breathe.

Witness yourself, and speak up. Sing like a canary, or even like an old crow. Just let your song loose in the world. Allow your lover to have whatever reaction your lover has – breathe and let it go – and keep on spilling the beans. Listen, you've got this life to live. Make it real, make it wonderful. Bring yourself out of hiding. *Speak Your Truth*. It's time. And the truth really will set you free.

In this chapter, *Law V: Speak Your Truth* we've covered:

- People lie about themselves in relationship because they fear they are "unlovable".

- True intimacy can only flourish when you are willing to tell the truth about your inner self.

- You cannot control your partner's response to your revelations and it is critical that you be truthful.

- Speaking up isn't the worst thing you can do in a relationship – keeping silent is.

- *Emotional Release* by yourself can help you express your truth in healthy, non-destructive ways when you are with your partner.

- Respect for your own personal integrity will help you love yourself more and expand your capacity to love.

   Now were ready to move on to the next law of Tantric Intimacy, *Law VI: Set Your Boundaries*. This next chapter will help you understand that even though you are being encouraged to be open, truthful, and honest in your relationships, you are also permitted to honor your own space and feelings within relationships, and must also respect those of your partner in order for true intimacy to flourish.

Law VI
Set Your Boundaries

The purpose of having boundaries is to protect and take care of ourselves. We need to be able to tell other people when they are acting in ways that are not acceptable to us. A first step is starting to know that we have a right to protect and defend ourselves; that we have not only the right, but the duty to take responsibility for how we allow others to treat us.

– Robert Burney

Some of you reading this book are going to see the title of this chapter and know instantly that setting boundaries is your most important issue. You know you don't honor your own space and your own feelings, and you know it's because of other people's reactions. You may not use the term "boundaries", but you're already talking to yourself (or yelling at yourself) about saying no when what you feel is *no* and yes when what you feel is *yes*. Being clear about what feels right for you, even when other people protest, is what it means to *Set Your Boundaries*.

My Space, Your Space

Setting boundaries might sound like *Speaking Your Truth*, but it's not quite the same. It's more intimate, closer into your personal space and sense of privacy. Setting boundaries is my own personal challenge, by the way. My partners have let me know, in no uncertain terms, that boundary-setting is my pet issue. I've probably had to do more work on myself regarding this law than just about anything else. I come across strong and I am strong, but the sixth law, *Set Your Boundaries*, has been my most difficult personal challenge.

I started out not being able to set boundaries with people and not being able to hear it when they set boundaries with me. What a pickle! One of the earliest examples I can remember is trying to prevent my parents from barging into my room unannounced all the time. In my house, I couldn't just say, "Please don't barge into my room unannounced", and expect that request to be honored. First, I'd get a lot of flack and accusations. Second, they wouldn't listen anyway. So I put a bell in the entryway for them to ring when they were approaching. In that way I'd hear *ding dong* and wouldn't be startled when the door just flew open. This early family experience has resulted in my tremendous respect for closed doors. It is probably the reason I don't like unannounced visitors. My personal preference for people to call before coming over is a perfect example of what boundaries are all about.

Boundaries are not universal. They vary according to each individual's needs and preferences. You have a right to set them for yourself, and you must also make sure that if living with someone, even married to them, you both maintain your own. In fact, rather than being a barrier to healthy intimacy, each having their own boundaries actually fosters it. You seek to protect your boundaries while respecting your partner's.

Sounds Like a Personal Problem

The purpose of setting boundaries is to show honor and respect for your personal space – physically, emotionally, and sexually. When you set boundaries, you assert the right to keep out what you don't want and to let in what you do want. They are like permeable cellular membranes, keeping out toxins and letting in nutrients. Naturally, everyone in your life seems to press into where your boundaries are, just like you press in on theirs. You may be unaware of your boundaries and of their boundaries, yet setting them is strictly a personal matter. It may be necessary to do a little self-awareness work to tune in to your own boundary signals, since boundaries are nothing more, or less, than what feels right to *you*. By the way, don't expect your partner to sort this out for you. You are involved in the dance of intimacy with them, but the boundaries you set are your responsibility alone. I'll talk more about how to tune into and clarify your boundaries later in the chapter.

Better Than a Donut Hole, But ...

Some of you know you aren't great with your boundaries, yet you're not sure how to improve. Others of you might have no idea how difficult it is for you to set clear boundaries, and aren't aware that boundary issues are behind many of your relationship upsets. That might be because of childhood experiences, which got you into trouble with your family, and made you feel unlovable or "wrong".

Examples of normal boundary-setting – which kids try to do naturally – could be drawing a line in the sand, not kissing a certain relative, trying to pick your own clothes, closing your bedroom door, or refusing to share your toys. These attempts aren't always too popular with grown-ups, so early on you picked some kind of protective strategy to get by, and decades later you're still living a version of it.

The thing about protective strategies is that they do the trick to some extent. They may not be the healthiest choices, but you had to find something that worked then, and you did. So now your strategy might be choosing partners who do all the boundary-setting for the relationship; all you have to do is smile and nod. On the other hand, you might be the one setting every limit for both of you – sure, it's a lot of work, but at least you get to be in total control. Or you might choose to live alone so you never have to deal with the issue at all.

Maybe you pick people whose demands overshadow yours, and that way never have to voice what it is *you* want. Or perhaps you've decided to be agreeable. Oh yes, you're so easy-going, so okay with everything (except for the constant, secret criticizing you're doing there in the back of your mind)! Or maybe, like me, you come across strong, so strong that people don't know how weak your boundaries are under all that tough talk.

I've been given the feedback that my protective strategy is to scare off "would be" boundary violators. Afraid that I won't be able to stand up for my own space and my own needs, I scare certain people off before they can even put me to the test. (That's what I meant before about coming across strong.) Please realize that for a long time, striking first may have been the only boundary-enforcing tool in my toolbox. As a protective strategy it has its drawbacks, but in the absence of other strategies, it kept me safe.

In your early years, you probably developed protective strategies that helped to maintain your boundaries, but now that you're grown, it may be time for a change into a more adult mode. Just look at your most recent intimate relationships – can you see what your boundaries, or lack of them, have been?

What Boundary Upset?

Here's an example, of a boundary upset scenario that happens to people quite often. Let's say you're hanging out with your lover, going with the flow, everything's good, no real problems on the horizon. Then, because it's human nature (and because you don't learn anything without problems to solve), your honey does something to violate one of your boundaries. All of a sudden you're not having much fun anymore. You're not sure what exactly set you off, though, or why. Since you don't know what to do, you immediately go to everyone's favorite defense – acting cool. On the surface you appear calm. At the most you withdraw a bit or get irritable. Then, if the event continues or happens again, suddenly, without warning, you snap. Yowza! Red alert! Watch out!

I was exactly like that before doing Tantra. What I didn't realize is that my yelling and screaming – and the feelings of betrayal and grief underneath the yelling and screaming – were all because I was afraid to make a simple request of the people closest to me at the early stages of a boundary violation. Whatever the underlying upset was, I couldn't address it directly. So I'd let it go and let it go and then, when I got to a certain level of discomfort, ka-boom!

> Another example of boundary upset is provided by Karin: "I can't tell you how many times I've left a job, a city, a group of friends, even a health club because there was someone there I couldn't set boundaries with. Rather than ask a person to back off or tell a man I wasn't interested, rather than reveal to a friend that some incident had hurt my feelings, I'd just leave. My idea of setting boundaries was to move several states away."

Lots of you never set a boundary until the moment you're ending a relationship, furious and destructive because your unstated and frequently unknown boundaries were violated. It's a funny thing, but your boundaries feel obvious to you. This is true even if you never defined them and never talked about them. Trust me on this: most of the time, your partner has no idea he or she has crossed the line of your personal space. Other people are worried about themselves and their feelings; you're worried about yourself and your own feelings. Nonetheless, you often feel like the other person violated your boundaries "on purpose", when in reality, they didn't even know they were there. And most likely neither did you.

Boundaries versus Barriers

Explaining simply and calmly, in a non-blaming way, exactly what your boundaries are, especially when you're feeling angry or hurt, is the best way to communicate with your partner. Instead what you probably do is tell yourself to get over it. (Something in people's upbringing makes them feel ashamed to have "boundary issues").

First you try to push your feelings down. Then you tell yourself why you're a big loser for being upset about something that other people would blow off. Next you dwell for a while on what a big loser your friend is for even doing that to you and not noticing your feelings. Finally you tell yourself, "Oh, saying anything isn't worth it. Nothing will change and I'll look stupid and everyone will be upset. I just need to keep my mouth shut or get different friends." That's how, day after day, you fail to respect your own boundaries. Essentially, you betray yourself in order to keep the peace. Externally, at least. Inwardly, you rage, fume, and steam. Or withdraw into yourself still further.

The fall-out from betraying yourself over and over again accumulates. You begin to guard yourself against possible hurts. You become suspicious of other people's motives. You stock up reptile brain's arsenal until you find yourself armored to the teeth. Rather than simple boundaries, you may discover you have barriers instead. This is hardly conducive to intimacy.

While boundaries can function to facilitate communication and relationships, barriers function like blockades. Nothing can get in or out of a barrier, not even the good stuff you desire, and letting go of the toxins becomes almost impossible. Barriers keep you feeling distant from others, even if you're living in the same house. Interestingly, you might not be aware that you've erected barriers, and you wonder why you've spent your life emotionally distant and far away from intimacy.

Whose Turn is It to Watch the Boundaries Tonight?

With so much anger and betrayal in relationships stemming from long-overlooked boundary violations, laying those feelings on your partner is almost irresistible. "I've told him again and again not to open the bathroom door but he never listens." Uh-huh. My response to that is, "Explain what you want, give him one chance, and then lock the bathroom door." You don't have to be mean about it. Do it with a kiss and a smile, but make your word your law. It's as simple as that, and also as hard as that. Remember, it's *your* job to mind your boundaries. Your lover's job is to respect your boundaries. And you get to respect his or hers in return.

If you say you'll lock the door from now on, and then you don't, what message are you putting out there? You're saying, "I can't hold myself to my own boundaries, but if you love me you'll do it for me." However, you're also saying, whether you mean to or not, "Since I don't respect my own boundaries, you don't have to either." That leads inevitably to the old refrain, "You don't respect my boundaries, so I guess you don't love me. I guess nobody loves me. I guess I'm just unlovable."

Some *Emotional Clearing* may be called for when you feel your boundaries are slipping, or have been violated. Then, when you're less reactive, maybe you can employ the witness technique and look at the situation more calmly. Your boundary is that you want privacy in the bathroom, and you don't feel loved when that boundary is violated. Your partner's boundary is that people who love each other should share the bathroom, so your boundary makes your partner feel unloved. Oh geez, talk about a pickle! If only there were some way of resolving this dilemma ...

A List of Common Boundaries

Here are some of the boundary issues I've come across in my life. You may have others to add to this list:

- Borrowing my things without returning them.

- Not asking if I have time to talk on the phone now, or not asking when would be a good time.

- Interrupting before I finish what I'm saying.

- Standing too close to me or standing too far away.

- Not looking at me when I'm talking.

- Being late.

- Not respecting my alone time or need for privacy.

- Having sex when I don't want to.

- Reading my journal without permission.

- Going through my possessions, wallet, pockets, drawers without permission.

- Giving me advice or coaching without asking if I want it.

If You Love Me, You'll Let Me

When you were a child, you couldn't stop the adults who sometimes dangerously violated your boundaries. Now that you're an adult, when you allow a boundary violation, the first thing that happens is far from a sane and balanced, grown-up repair job. No, generally you revert to childhood coping mechanisms. You freeze up. Your stomach hurts or your hands get numb. You stop having fun and you hate yourself. You may even leave your body. You burst into tears or maybe you start kicking and screaming in self-protection. Whatever your preferred method is, basically you freak out in a way that comes from a much younger time in your life.

The truth is that there's a very good chance your partner will freak out too when you set a boundary. There's a very good chance that you'll freak out when your partner sets one with you. It's because everyone thinks that saying no is the same thing as saying I don't love you. You think a boundary equals a rejection. Or maybe you think, because of the way you were raised, that you don't have the right to set boundaries at all, and neither does anyone else. This confuses the rights and responsibilities you each have concerning your boundaries.

Rights and Responsibilities

As I stated earlier, it is not your lover's job to be the watchdog of your boundaries. Your boundaries are *your* responsibility. If you can't say no to something and mean it, why should your partner do it for you? Stop and examine your beliefs. Why do you betray yourself and second-guess your boundaries? Do you think that betraying your boundaries will make your partner happy? What is it that you hope to gain by sacrificing yourself anyway? Why do you let these violations go on unchecked, and does it really help your relationship? How do you feel about your partner if he or she just lets you walk all over his or her boundaries? Do you think it fosters respect, intimacy, growing closer? Or will it activate reptile brain's instincts of fight, flight or freeze?

Shoot, I Had Those Boundaries Here a Second Ago ...

From my own experience I can verify that it's very difficult to simply state your boundaries and requests (see the chapter on *Please Yourself*). Standard operating procedure is to wait until you're so angry that speaking up is not the issue, but rather a question of whether you can control your reactions so as not to psychically kill off the other person (or yourself). So the flip side of that reptile-brain anger – feeling victimized, and all that pitiful-me stuff – is really just the same thing. You're still trying to get people to respect your boundaries without your having to say what the hell those boundaries are calmly, clearly, and without apology.

Having clear boundaries to begin with is helpful. In other words, to respect them properly, you have to know your boundaries. Dang it, where are those suckers? The body already knows, but the mind keeps interfering. The mind has opinions about whether the boundaries are acceptable or not, about whether they'll be acceptable to other people or not, and about whether you can honor them and still keep the status quo. You learned long ago to tune out your natural boundary signals. Now you have to do some remedial work. In the same way you have to check inside yourself to *Speak Your Truth*, you'll have to learn to check inside to *Set Your Boundaries*.

The Right to Choose

Until you give yourself permission to have boundaries, everything in the world is going to come at you and enter your space. As long as that's going on, a part of you might feel victimized. When you consciously choose for yourself, without apology or blame, you can find real bliss in relationship. When you see clearly what is and isn't okay with you – and you honor that boundary – then you can invite pleasure in. Once you let pleasure into your life, you can invite love in as well.

Giving yourself the right to choose what you want and don't want in your life is a very powerful and self-loving place to be. It's the place where intimacy thrives. To go a step further, once there really is trust in a relationship, the boundaries can be renegotiated. In other words, maybe the bathroom door can be left ajar once in awhile. Boundaries soften when there is true heart and soul connection, with mutual respect for each other's boundaries.

Ground Rules

Touching is the external, visible manifestation of your inner boundary life. As part of the ground rules in the courses I teach, I request that people refrain from touching each other automatically. I require course participants to ask permission to touch, unless touching is a specific instruction for one of the exercises in the course. This rule applies especially to couples who participate together. After years of bypassing boundary signals in an effort to get along in romantic relationships, boundaries are usually muddiest with the people you're closest to. Again, just because you live together or are even married, does not mean you are not both entitled to boundaries with regards to body, space, possessions, money and so on.

In my workshops I give permission to experiment with the notion of boundaries in a safe environment. I let people find out that nobody dies from hearing the word "no." In this vein, even at home I strongly suggest you ask to touch, ask to hug, ask to kiss. See how it feels in each moment, rather than operating in an automatic way with an arm thrown around the shoulder. Then you can make your inevitable mistakes and clean them up, as well as find out where your and other people's boundaries are.

When you're practicing at home, practice a little bit on harmless topics. Your goal is to set a clear boundary and stand by it without wanting to either die from guilt or to murder from rage. Keep it reasonable. Ask to have the television on more quietly. Mention that you'd like help with the dishes. You'll have to do it more than once, by the way, so don't lose heart if your first effort fizzles. Notice something that's out of alignment about your boundaries and make a request about it. If you can't, then tune in to your body and Be Your Own Witness for a while. Practice some Emotional Release. Then, when you're ready, try speaking up again. And again. Which is not the same as nagging, but simply expressing your inner truth.

Accentuate the Positive

One tip I have to add here is to focus on what you do want, rather than on what you don't want. Whatever you put your focus and energy on is usually what you get. The more you focus on what you don't want, the more power it gets. Once you distinguish what you do want, focus on that. Speak it; ask for it; refine it. Stop speaking the rest of the story altogether. This is what is meant by the phrase, "Think positively". Speak positively as well.

I am not advising you to deny when something feels wrong, not at all. If necessary, put your hand up and say simply, "Wait a moment." (See the section below on "The Power to Stop"). Take a minute to express what you want in positive terms. Instead of saying, "I hate you for interrupting me," say, "I want to finish what I'm saying before you begin to speak. Can you honor that?" Do you see the difference?

The Power to Stop

Checking in with yourself and your boundaries is something you will have to do for the rest of your life. This gets easier with practice, but if you're dealing with other human beings you will always be negotiating and re-negotiating boundaries. Sometimes there are going to be mistakes, intentional and unintentional ones. So what happens when there's a boundary violation? What do you do when you realize that you agreed to something that isn't actually okay with you? What about when you think you did that to someone else?

First of all, STOP. Whatever's going on, just stop it. Stop right there and speak your truth. It doesn't have to be elegant; it doesn't have to be strong or decisive or witty or anything else. It doesn't have to be okay by other people. It only has to be *your* truth. If all you can manage is one word, just say, "Stop." That's enough. Then, when you can, state your boundary and make your request. You can even say, "I have a boundary about that." This makes things very clear between you.

On the bright side, it's never too late to reset your boundaries. It's never too late to clear up a boundary incident. Sure, it would be nice if you could speak up in the moment of the violation, but it is perfectly okay to speak up whenever you're ready. If that's three years down the line, so be it. Don't let the fear of foolishness stop you. Spill the beans. Speak up. You'll get that weight out of your cells, you'll get the benefit of the emotional release, and your body will appreciate you for it, no matter when it happens.

Beyond the Beyond

To practice boundary-setting in a pleasurable way, in my *Ecstasy* course I create a ritual dinner called the *Gate Dinner* (pronounced Gah-tay). Gate translated from Sanskrit means "beyond". Participants begin by practicing a few responses to a request: "No, not now," "No, never," "No, not like that," "Yes, I'd like that," "Yes, but I need a moment," or "Oh, I changed my mind."

At the opening of the Gate Dinner we chant an ancient Sanskrit chant: *Gate gate para gate, para sum gate, bodhi swaha.* (Gone beyond, beyond the beyond, hail the awakened one.). It is Buddha's mantra, the *Heart of Wisdom Sutra.* After we recite the chant, I lead a guided visualization during which the women and men see themselves as goddesses and gods about to participate in a sacred feast. (Imagine the ancient gods of Greece and Rome, treating each other with honor and respect, along with a mix of playfulness.) Then, in a special way, we feast.

During the ritual of the Gate Dinner, people play with permission for varying degrees of pleasure while experimenting with boundaries. The dinner itself consists of many courses, beginning with breaking family rules by having luscious chocolate dessert first! The goddesses are seated at permanent stations around the banquette table. The gods rotate around to different goddesses from course to course. During each course the gods offer to feed each new goddess while experimenting with boundaries. For example, a god might ask, "May I feed you mango from my inner thigh?", or "May I eat strawberries off the nape of your neck?" The response from the goddess may be any of those mentioned above, from "No, never," to "No, not now, maybe later," to "Yes, I'd love that!"

Nothing Personal

Everyone at the Gate Dinner has been coached ahead of time to understand that boundaries are to be respected at the same time as they are to be experimented with in play mode. The gods and goddesses are instructed not to take any response personally. Participants in this feast respond from an empowered position. If the goddess says Yes, then the god goes for it. If she says No, he doesn't take it personally. Her boundaries are hers. Also, he knows there are many other courses at this dinner and many other stations where he will get to play with other goddesses and other foods.

This is a tremendously eye-opening experiment for most people. Many participants learn to relax and be true to themselves during this playful exercise. Some hate it. It poses the challenge of taking complete responsibility for pleasure and fun, while at the same time taking complete responsibility for comfort and boundaries.

Set up a Gate Dinner of your own for you and your partner, with festive, sensuous foods. Have an opening ritual. Put on beautiful music. Then begin to ask for permission to feed your lover from different places on your body, or to eat a particular food off your partner's sensuous body areas. Be playful. See how you can open up this communication about boundaries and pleasure.

> Sheri said this of herself and her new fiancé after taking the Butterfly Tantra courses, "Rather than assuming the other wants to be hugged, touched or even have sex, we've practiced asking a lot. I don't take it personally anymore if he says, "No" or "Not like that." I'm getting better at asking for what I want and saying what I don't want. The communication between us is great."

Ask First

The key to boundary work with your beloved is to make sure you ask. After you ask, make sure you listen. The most honoring and tender thing you can do for your lover is to listen properly, without inserting yourself into your partner's space. Make room for your lover to answer, and then don't take the answer personally. Respect his or her space as you would wish your own to be respected.

> William, who moved in with the woman of his dreams after taking many of the courses offered through Butterfly Workshops, wrote this beautiful piece about learning boundaries:

She needs more space. I become an architect of space.
I need to be close. She becomes a seamstress of space.

You can probably understand this concept when you apply it to someone you love. Now apply it to boundary work with yourself. Ask yourself what's going on with you. Ask yourself what you want. Ask yourself if you like this. Ask yourself if you want to keep going. Then *listen* to the answer. It may not be what you expected. Tough luck! Honor it anyway. If you can do that with yourself, you can do it with your lover. If you can honor your lover, you can honor yourself. It's reciprocal. It's a positive feedback loop.

So remember to ask, and remember to listen. When you *Set Your Boundaries*, you open the door to pleasure that will continue for the rest of your life. Life is meant to be enjoyed, and setting your boundaries is part of that enjoyment. Setting boundaries allows you to feel safe, secure, respected, valued, so you can live fully, embracing all of life as you will see in the next section, *Law VII: The Mirror of Your Beloved*

But before we move on, let's just go over *Law VI: Set Your Boundaries*:

- Boundaries are a healthy way of owning your feelings and space and respecting your own inner truth.

- Everyone has the right to set their own boundaries.

- Everyone has the right to have their boundaries respected.

- There is a difference between boundaries and barriers. One supports healthy relationships, the other halts them.

- Both partners in a relationship are responsible for their own boundaries, but not each other's.

- Respect yourself enough to maintain your boundaries and flexible enough to know they may change over time and from one relationship to another.

- Ask permission regarding another's boundaries, such as touch.

- Don't take another's boundaries personally.

Law VII
The Mirror of Your Beloved

Love is like a mirror. When you love another you become his mirror and he becomes yours ... And reflecting each other's love you see infinity.

— Leo Buscaglia

The meeting of two personalities is like the contact of two chemical substances: if there is any reaction, both are transformed.

— Carl Jung

Love takes off masks that we fear we cannot live without and know we cannot live within.

— James Baldwin

Most of you believe deep down that you have no real control over who you fall in love with. You think love happens because of something like a rogue Cupid's dart – zap! – and there you are, out of your mind with love and lust and dreams of the future.

Have I Been Here Before?

First you're crazily in love; next thing you know you're driving each other to the brink. Or, I don't know, maybe you went the practical route. First you're congratulating yourself on how sensible you were to have picked this perfectly presentable person; next thing you know, you're wondering if your head was ever screwed on straight.

In either case, you start analyzing everything and end up kicking yourself. You're in yet another situation so reminiscent of your parents (and/or your past six relationships) that you could just scream. When you try to figure out what attracted you in the first place, and then what went so damn wrong, it seems to have happened with no rhyme or reason at all.

In Tantra, though, there's a rhyme and a reason for everything. In Tantra, the reason behind every situation is that the universe wants you to evolve and live fully embracing it all. Looking into *The Mirror of Your Beloved* is a way to realize that every single thing driving you so nuts about your lover is really just a lesson for you waiting to happen. Every upset – if you can get past the upset – is an opportunity for you to learn something worthwhile about yourself and about love.

Hey Sweetie, Step on My Last Nerve

As far as partner-picking goes, you unconsciously pick partners who push the buttons you hate – yet need – to have pushed. They don't push those buttons right away, of course (they're too busy pushing the delicious ones first), but they'll push them eventually. Why? For the good reason that you're here to grow, to transform, and to live with near-mythic mind-altering intimacy and love. In order to achieve the mind-altering intimacy and love part, however, you first have to slay (or befriend) many a dragon. Since most of the dragons live only inside your head, they can be tricky bastards. Your lovers are drawn to you, and you to them, to bring those beasts out into the open.

In the cosmic sense, you come together to confront your darkest fears and deepest secrets, both psychologically and spiritually. You are drawn to certain people ostensibly because of their great smiles or how they look in a bikini, but that's not why you enter into relationships. You form deep and powerful connections with certain attractive human beings because they are the medium through which you confront your true fears and most shameful secrets.

It may sound like fun (not!), but this is hardly what date movies are about. It's not even what your dating life is about, usually. The dragons are there from the start, but they tend to hide for a while behind pheromones and excitement and the facades we talked about in Tantric Intimacy Law V: *Speak Your Truth*.

Time for the Cold Shower

You might think it's your lover's job to love you. Ha! In the cosmic, transformational, Tantric spiritual sense, it's actually your lover's job to stop you cold and make you look at every bad habit you have, every self-pitying proclamation, every story about your own failures, and every excuse you make about your life. If your lover has a job in relation to you, that job is to shock you into awareness of how much growing up you still have to do. How? By irritating you, disappointing you, and breaking your heart ... by pushing every fake, self-pitying, angry, blaming, untransformed button you possess ... by making you think how fake and self-pitying and untransformed your lover is.

It's a cosmic joke. While you're taking aim at your partner and finding fault, you're actually highlighting the areas in which *you* need to grow. And learning how to be more loving and forgiving of yourself, and thus more loving and forgiving of others.

Broadly speaking, you learned how to manage relationships, good and bad, from your parents. They had their dark fears and deep secrets too. Did they confront them? Did they learn from them? Did they grow in passion and compassion because of them?

Unfortunately for most people, the working model of happily-ever-after was a choice between *Sleeping Beauty* and *The Donna Reed Show*. In other words, you weren't given too many tools to manage the real world of love. The difference that Tantra makes is that where my parents, for example, may have refused to look at their fears or denied that they existed, I run towards mine. Tantra has allowed me to see my fears clearly and then embrace them, knowing that nothing is wrong with me. What a relief!

In my case, my parents pretty much disagreed about everything raising my sister and me. They disagreed about how to manage money, what to tell the children about sex, whether to practice religion and much, much more. They gave us their messages separately, and sometimes even fought about what one or the other had told us. I felt that I pretty much had to fend for myself.

I definitely didn't want their relationship. In fact, I was driven to do anything I could to be different from them. The crazy thing is that I turned out to have lots of the characteristics in them I couldn't stand. What a revelation! I found this out by painfully looking into the *Mirror of My Beloved*. Boy, sometimes I wanted to break the mirror.

More Than Sex?

I imagine you're looking at this book because you want more than what your parents had (or maybe they had it good, and you haven't figured out yet how they did it). You want real intimacy. You want good sex, easy laughter, and freedom of self-expression. Or maybe you just want to get laid a lot. I don't know your motives. You might not even know them yourself. Tantra will help lay them bare, if you do the practices.

I should tell you that Tantra is about much more than sex. That's why this book is about more than sex. This is a book about mind-blowing intimacy and the self-love that is required in order to enable yourself to open to letting that kind of love into your life. We only get that kind of passionate intimacy from plunging into the depths of our souls. That requires us to look at things in a different way. Tantra offers a different paradigm for life than most of us were taught, and moving into that paradigm requires courage.

Metamorphosis

The caterpillar builds the pupa around itself and then the pupa hardens to form a chrysalis. Once the chrysalis is formed, liquid cells (which we would probably call cancer) begin to devour the cells of the caterpillar. When the caterpillar has been changed entirely into the liquid, the liquid then begins to take yet another solid form. That new form is the butterfly.

I once spent a day with the butterfly expert at the Smithsonian, and I asked him if the caterpillar has a choice whether to become or not become a butterfly. "No," said the butterfly expert. "The caterpillar has to transform. It's in the DNA."

It's my belief that people have to transform too, just like the caterpillar. Nothing is permanent. Everything is in a constant state of change. Most people kid themselves into thinking things can stay the same. In fact, it is our resistance to change that causes our troubles, not the change itself.

For example, if your partner keeps pulling away and playing the distance game, maybe your partner is afraid of intimacy. Or maybe your way of going through life, which is to push and push for what you want, is not working. You could hate your lover and feel unworthy of affection. Or you could learn something from your lover's response and (get ready for this) try something new.

I'm OK, You're OK

Consider something radical. Consider that there is actually nothing wrong with you AND nothing wrong with your lover. Everything happening in your relationship is all just a kind of classroom, the milieu in which you get to learn something about yourself that would otherwise remain hidden and untransformed. Good news, huh?

What I'm saying is that there's nothing intrinsically "wrong" with your partner even if, for example, he or she is constantly on the make. It's just a different way of viewing the world. (And remember that your partner too is viewing relationships from the perspective of the childhood lessons he or she was exposed to through his or her family dynamic.) There is nothing wrong with the fact that you don't have money together or can't stand each other's friends. There is nothing wrong with being alone. There is nothing wrong with being scared that your spouse will get you in trouble, that you disguise your true feelings and thoughts, that you feel isolated and angry, or that your partner is mean and won't sleep with you. Even if you drink too much or you bury yourself in the television, there's really nothing *wrong*. You aren't a rat or a weakling. Your lover isn't a jerk. There are no lost causes...

In Tantra we distinguish between a person and their actions. Everyone is precious and to be cherished, no matter what their actions. Everyone makes mistakes. And these are all interpretations anyway. What is good to one person, like chocolate, could be bad to another. Right, wrong, self, other, these are all only words, labels, and all a question of one's own individual perspective.

Respect your own perspective, require that yours be respected by others, and respect other's, and sometimes agree to disagree. The world would be an awfully dull place if we all agreed on everything, wouldn't it?

As we discussed in the previous two Tantric Laws of Intimacy, *Law V: Speak your Truth* and *Law VI: Set Your Boundaries,* our feelings and opinions about ourselves very much depend on what our family and society at large have taught us to think about our feelings and emotions. The more you think about yourself or things in your life as if there's something terribly wrong, the more you're going to get twisted up about yourself or them. Getting twisted up and attached doesn't help you problem-solve; instead, it just gets you locked into the same old patterns that got you here in the first place. It's helpful to think of it all as being reflections in the cosmic mirror, not good or bad, just interesting situations giving you another opportunity for transformation. Witness, feel, learn, and grow.

Same Ol' Misery and the Blah Blah Blah

Of course, you have to look with open eyes and an open heart to see this, because I don't mean "observe, criticize, attack and condemn". I'm not telling you to beat yourself up because you chose the partner you chose, or because you behave the way you behave. I'm definitely not telling you to go on a long jag about what a loser you are for putting yourself in the same situation again and again, and what's wrong with you that no one in your life loves you right, and blah blah blah.

I'm not kidding; it's all just blah blah blah. It's those hostile reptile brain voices attacking you when you're down, or attacking your lover when you're both down, managing to keep everything *just the way it is.* You might be miserable, but at least you're on safe and familiar ground, right? That's what reptile brain wants. It protects and preserves itself by trying to keep things exactly the same.

So what do you do to get out of this mess? Well, first you witness it without comment, without judgment. You can even witness how hard it is for you to do that. Look and see how you feel about not blaming yourself for your life, about letting up on the clamp of self-condemnation. I don't know why, but finding someone to blame is like handing a kid a favorite blanket; it's such a comfort. See if you notice yourself doing that. Are you looking for a scapegoat? Who are you using as a scapegoat, and why?

Now look and see how you feel about not blaming your lover or your children or your parents for the mess all around you. Maybe it's no one's fault. Maybe nothing's as wrong as you think. Relax for a minute. Breathe in through the nose and out through the mouth, making a sigh. What happens if it's no one's fault and there's really nothing wrong? In what ways does this free you? In what ways does this empower you?

Should I Stay or Should I Go?

The Mirror of Your Beloved says that ditching this partner for someone new and improved isn't necessarily going to solve anything. Mind you, I'm not saying you have to stay together, either. Only you can answer that question.

What I am saying is not to do anything hasty. And that as long as you're reactive, angry, and locked-up about things in relation to your partner, you haven't learned yet what you need to learn together. Cosmically speaking, there's a lesson you need to get that this person is providing, and you'll know you've learned it when you can move again, or move on with clarity, love and compassion.

I mean that sincerely. Until you feel true compassion and love (and possibly even gratitude) for the worst, most damaging person in your life, you will find yourself facing versions of that same person in the same mirror again and again and again, for as long as you live. Dump your current partner or friend and you will find that, no matter how you try, your next partner or friend will do his or her own versions of exactly the things that are driving you to such despair now.

Do you find yourself in yet another unhappy relationship because you can't help being attracted to awful people? No. Does it happen because you're a magnet for abuse and you always will be? No. No, no, no. It happens because you've got your beautifully individualized lessons to learn in this lifetime, and until you learn them, you'll be like Bill Murray in *Groundhog Day,* repeating your life over and over and over again.

Bliss is as much a state of mind as a state of being. Everyone wants to be happy, to have meaningful, harmonious, even passionately vibrant relationships, with friends, family, lovers. Ask yourself: are you allowing yourself to be truly open to the possibility of bliss?

In Tantra the belief is that the universe wants you to get it, *it* being your particular lesson. The universe will therefore provide endless opportunities for this learning to take place. The point of all this is not to punish or torture you, but rather to open your eyes to your limitless potential and capacity for bliss and ecstasy. There is no fault in another that you don't share, and no virtue that you don't express. Open your eyes so you can embrace it all – everything in life.

The alternative is to keep on blaming the other person (or your divorced parents, or your lousy bone structure, or your boss) for your unhappiness as much as you want. But this strategy hasn't worked so far, now has it? So when you're ready to knuckle down and evolve, look in the mirror. You've got something to learn at the soul level. Everyone does. So put on your thinking cap and think. Pull on your feeling clothes and feel. Ask yourself over and over, "What am I doing to cause this?" or "Why am I choosing this situation?" "What is it I need to see?" When you come up with an answer that really makes you squirm, relax and breathe – you're getting close.

Your Own Beeswax

By the way, a caveat of this law is to look for your *own* lessons in life. You're not out here to look for other people's lessons, okay? They're here to do that for themselves. No matter how smart and insightful you think you are, turn that talent toward the demystifying of your own behavior, rather than to the analysis of your partner's behavior. You're here to figure out your own path and to clean up your own mistakes. Maybe other people have multitudinous problems and sins, but in this lifetime you have enough of your own to keep you busy for the rest of it. Trust me.

Listen and Learn

Your secret hatred and your secret resentment and your secret unhappiness are not secrets at all. They're strategies. They are a way to keep you stockpiling weapons in your reptile brain's arsenal, and the people closest to you in your life *know* what you're doing. You aren't fooling anyone. If your lovers aren't bringing up the issues, it's because they're avoiding their own lessons, or not speaking their truth. Possibly the two of you have struck an agreement – they'll go easy on you if you go easy on them. (e.g. You won't bring up her obsessive shopping sprees if she doesn't bring up how much you work.)

In truth, you're mirroring each other's lessons whether you choose to deal consciously with them or not. Take a look. What are you avoiding bringing up to yourself or your significant other? Which reptile brain in the relationship is going to have the courage to propose a disarmament treaty?

Joan shared: In my marriage, which was really struggling, I finally saw something about how desperately I didn't want to take care of myself in the real world. Even my previous fiancé was furious with me about that, but I couldn't even talk about it in those days. Then I married Jeff and started to take care of everything in the world except making decent money. He had to quit working for two years before I really stepped up to the plate as a financially viable human being. I never would have done that if he had kept working, kept going with things the way they were. Given my choice, I probably would never have grown up. Now, I would never go back to the way it was before. So really, in the deepest part of me, I'm grateful for what he showed me about myself and forced me to confront.

I don't know what your lessons are, but you do. Down on the soul level you know things that you may not know up in your brain. The thing you're hoping it isn't is probably what it *is*. Remember, your partner is your mirror, reflecting back at you every lesson you need to learn. Look hard. Open your eyes wide. You wouldn't be together if you didn't have something to learn together. So go ahead, take your lover by the hand and figure it out together.

Does all this make love sound unromantic? Sorry! I meant it earlier when I said that nothing's *wrong*. You aren't wrong for accusing other people of faults that are actually your own. You aren't even wrong for being reactive and upset by their behavior. It's all just a learning opportunity for you, much like analyzing dreams. Your words, especially the ones you aren't entirely aware of as you speak them, are clues to your subconscious. Listen to what you're saying. Sometimes the thing you tell another person about them is what your subconscious is trying to tell you about you, so listen up. The *Mirror of Your Beloved* may not be as pretty as a fairy tale ending, but it is a great place to evolve. Both for yourself, and for the passionate relationship you always wanted to have. Mirror, mirror on the wall...

To reinforce many of the points I've raised in this chapter, let's take a look at Sheila's story:

Sheila confesses: I was drawn to Tantra once I was divorced. I had been married for 12 years, and it had been a terrific marriage in all respects except the physically intimate. That had been partly to do with physical illness. We had dated for 6 months with all the passion and fire anyone could ever have hoped for. Then he was diagnosed with testicular cancer, and things were never really the same after that. We married at once to brave his illness together, and shortly after that, I had a very serious miscarriage. Then he had surgery, and chemotherapy.

We loved, admired and respected each other, but things were never the same after I lost the baby. Once we were both on the road to physical recovery, I hoped we could go back to the way things had been, but I just got shut out most of the time whenever I tried to restore our previous intimacy. He had had one testicle removed, and suffered sickness from the chemotherapy. I tried not to feel resentful and sadden at the loss of our once-vibrant sex life. I kept telling myself that at least he was still alive, that every day I had with the man I loved was a gift, since death had come so close.

But once he was out of the woods, the cancer gone, the lack of sex started to feel a bit like a living death for me as a vibrant, feminine woman. I knew my partner had issues from his own ultra Catholic background. He had actually been a virgin when we met, though much older than me.

Sadly, I think he saw his cancer as a punishment in some way for the passion we had shared, so even though he was fully functional physically, emotionally he was closed down, and refused to even think about getting counseling. I tried to be natural with the man I loved, warm and affectionate, but he often took it as a violation of his boundaries, that merely holding hands was me trying to initiate sex. I tried to respect his boundaries, and not be too 'forward' in my desires the rare times when he did decide he wanted to make love.

We had everything in common, seemed to be the perfect couple in every respect, but I ached with grief for the kind of passion we had had in the early days before our respective illnesses. Yet I made do with occasional sex and a lot of self-love, and throwing myself into work. I lost the ability to orgasm with him, to the point where he even noticed, and was bothered enough by it to ask what he could do to please me. I lied and pretended I was pleased, or worse still, I lied and refused sex because it just seemed too depressing. The sex seemed nothing more than mechanical, a travesty of the superb lovemaking we had once shared, the vibrant vitality and joy in living that I longed for.

Then his father died, and the man I had lived with for 12 years vanished right before my eyes. He was angry, wild, out of control, began drinking, crashing our cars, using drugs, yelling at me, when he had never raised his voice in his life. I confronted him, and he walked out the door one day and never came back.

For all that I had gone through during my marriage, and at the end of it, I still had hope. I decided if I was ever going to have another relationship with a man, it would be on my terms. Those terms would be passion and intimacy, not frigidity and rejection.

I studied Tantra for 2 years before I dared risk dating, dared attempt to practice with a lover. Fate brought him to me the one and only time I ever stepped foot in a Starbuck's looking for, of all things, an herbal tea.

We shared a table, took the identical Tantra book out of our respective briefcases to read, and the rest, as they say, is history. The universe gifted me with my soul mate in the last place I could ever have imagined.

Through Tantric intimacy, we've learned together, and the love we've created has healed him just as much as it's healed me. Truthfully, I never imagined I would share my life with someone like him – he is the last person I would ever have thought of as my 'type.' And he has certainly never met anyone like me; every day we've shared in the past 2 years is just full of delightful surprises. He has learned to heal and trust for the first time, to know he is worthy of love, to set boundaries, not erect barriers, and finally has the courage to live his own inner truth and higher purpose.

I never thought it would be possible, but I now look at my divorce as the best thing that has ever happened to me, shaking me out of my sleep-walking life shattering my old patterns. Despite the absolute agony at the time, and the ongoing agony of my increasing sexual deprivation while I was married, the ecstasy that all my Tantric work has brought to my life (and that of my partner) would never have happened without that pain and suffering.

Like the butterfly breaking out of the cocoon, the transformation may be excruciating at times, but the act of breaking out brings the blood to the wings to help them spread so it can fly. The glory of our new lives and love is greater than anything we could ever have imagined. And even if we ever separate as lovers, ours souls have truly touched. Neither distance nor moving on to grow in separate ways can ever diminish or take away the true ecstasy we've found. While Tantric Intimacy does take work, both by myself and when we are together, I would never again settle for anything less than genuine intimate love in a relationship.

As I said above, the *Mirror of Your Beloved* may not be as pretty as a fairy tale ending, but it is a great place to evolve. You really can slay your inner dragons and find the intimacy you've always dreamed of.

Tantric Law of Intimacy VII: The Mirror of Your Beloved has opened up for you the ideas that:

- You choose partners according to the relationship patterns you witness in childhood, in our own families.

- The things that upset you most about romantic partners are often the things you need to work on within yourself.

- While you work on your stuff, let your partners work on theirs.

- Tantric intimacy welcomes and accepts it all, dark and light.

- Tantric intimacy takes work, but the passionate intimacy is well worth it.

With this last item in mind, and taking it in the positive spirit it's intended, let's move on to Tantric *Law VIII: Full Contact Confrontation.*

Law VIII

Full Contact Confrontation

Be still when you have nothing to say; when genuine passion moves you, say what you've got to say, and say it hot.
  – D. H. Lawrence

Fear not those who argue but those who dodge.
  – Marie Ebner von Eschenbach

Love is everything it's cracked up to be...It really is worth fighting for, being brave for, risking everything for.
  – Erica Jong

What I call *Full Contact Confrontation* is taking on a real fight to get to something bigger, even transcendent, in your relationship. Instead of sweeping a difficult issue under the rug because you brought it up before and got nowhere (or were shot down in flames), *Full Contact Confrontation* allows you to realize that not only have you reached the core issues in your relationship, but the dark force in you and the dark force in your lover have merged into a powerful and frightening codependent stranglehold. *Full Contact Confrontation* is a toe-to-toe and head-to-head battle, waged when your integrity or your well-being is at stake.

Drama, Demons, Destruction, Desire

Does this sound over-dramatic? It really isn't. I'm talking about the issues that are central to your story of you, issues that are the archetypal beasts rampaging through your psyche. Everyone has them, though not all admit it or know these beasts by name. Buried down inside you are your secret fears and ravenous needs. Buried in your lover are the complementary fears and needs. If those needs don't somehow coordinate and fit together – not always healthily, mind you – then you probably won't stay together long. The juice won't be there.

That's why some people are attractive but do nothing for you, whereas other people pull you in with an inexplicable force. Those beings who are so magnetic to you have a spiritual connection to your psyche. You've come together to work out big issues, issues that might have dogged you for lifetimes already. How do you recognize this? Oh, you'll be swimming along in love thinking golly gee, this is the best person you've ever known in all your life and then, . . . Shazam! Somebody pushes a button and the past comes rushing over you like an endless, repetitive nightmare. Yikes! That's when you know you've careened right into a previously snoozing inner demon.

Once you've hit one of these bad boys – after which your relationship will never be quite the same, by the way – you and your lover might fight all the time, yet challenge and change nothing in the relationship. Or you might bear down grimly and refuse to fight, also challenging and changing nothing in the relationship. These are only two of the possible ways people manage not to confront their issues. Numbing out with alcohol or television is another way, losing yourself in the children is standard, and overwork is yet another. Trying to talk about it and fading into awkward silence happens quite a lot, too. Everyone is so creative when it comes to avoidance!

Stormy Weather

In case this all sounds too much like hard work in a love relationship, believe me, it isn't, not compared with the alternative.

Full Contact Confrontation is not the petty squabbling and ugly bickering that sucks your energy yet keeps things (reassuringly) just the way they are. It's not about those civilized talks either, the ones that start out so promisingly, then change topic under pressure. I'm all in favor of at least trying to talk; however, *Full Contact Confrontation* is much more than talk. It's about going for the big fight when the big fight is necessary, and refusing to be drawn into little side conflicts that only distract from the real issue at hand. Rather than continuing your tacit agreement with each other not to rock the boat, *Full Contact Confrontation* is a choice to sail headlong into the storm.

As I've said before, intimacy in the deep Tantric sense isn't about having a nice relationship; it's about having a *real* relationship, and a real relationship comes from weathering the stormy seas together. Only when you go full contact and take on the huge nerve-wracking issues with your lover – issues such as lying, or alcoholism, infidelity, obesity, or your love life – can ecstatic intimacy truly become the basis for your relationship.

Is This the Way to Batten a Hatch?

I can hear you say, "Well okay, Laurie, if you say so, but how do you actually weather bad times? Won't your partner leave you first? Won't you run off with the mailman, or the preschool teacher? Should you really have to work so hard at love? And anyway, you can't force someone else to change. Didn't you say that already?"

I did say that, and you're right. You can't force someone else to change. You can't even force yourself to change, not inside, not at the level we're talking about. Profound transformation comes when you're ready for it, and not a moment before. Then it happens in an instant, faster than you can blink.

To get ready for that, though, you first have to respect your process. Nothing changes until you respect the place where you are now. When you see yourself clearly without shame and judgment *and* you see the people in your life more as a blessing, without shaming or judging, profound change is already underway.

I do want to remind you of something here. You can probably influence, but you can't control what your partner does or thinks or feels. You can't control how another person will react to your words. It's not even your business to try micromanaging that. *You* are your business, so when you come smack up against a mystifying wall in your relationship, the place you need to look for clues to the mystery is inside yourself.

The Process of the Process

In the act of observing Nature, Nature changes, but it doesn't change because you forced change. That's the power of *Being Your Own Witness*. But witness compassionately. Witness yourself with kindness.

This might take everything you've got. Notice when you find yourself kicking your car hard enough to bruise your toe. Let the red flags fly when you see that you've locked yourself in an upstairs bedroom at a party to hide. Wake up! Realize you've had sex like a crazed rabbit for ten years now and never even looked any of your lovers in the eye. In other words, *notice* what you're doing in this life. Really notice it, as if you were a stranger you were hired to watch. Practice seeing yourself clearly, and try doing it with a little tenderness.

It's important that you practice *Emotional Release* during this process, over and over and over. Let the memories come, as well as the grief, the rage, and the loneliness. Be there for yourself throughout this process. Even when you're just screaming in the car, honor your process, and *Honor Your* (wonderful, truth-telling) *Anger*.

As the words come to you and the knowledge grows, *Speak Your Truth*. It's okay if the truth changes for you; speak your truth about that too. Speaking your truth on a small-scale basis daily will let the real issues of your relationship come to light. Happily, as you become more adept at hearing what your body is telling you, you'll also be able to *Set Your Boundaries* more clearly. In other words, you'll feel safer in your skin. Then, when you feel ready, plunge headlong, *Full Contact Confrontation*, into the new adventure of bringing up and dealing with the really scary, risky stuff.

Full Contact Confrontation means opening yourself to everything in your experience. Use everything you know, everything you see, and most of all, everything you feel. Don't cover it over. Don't mask your experience. Don't numb out. *Full Contact Confrontation* means jumping out of the airplane with your parachute on your back. It means checking – or even chucking – your Bungee cord and launching yourself off the cliff. *Full Contact Confrontation* is deciding to bare yourself to the experience of really experiencing your life.

Eyes Wide Open

You'd be amazed at how much of life is geared toward letting you live without full awareness. You're trying all day long to escape actually *feeling* your life. That's because there's a lot of anxiety that accompanies the way people live these days. Most of what you buy, eat, watch, and say is done to escape anxiety. When I say jump *Full Contact* into a confrontation with your anxiety and fear, I know that I'm saying something huge.

Confront This

What I am actually saying is the confrontation you must face is with your *fear*; it's not with your partner. Whatever your partner is doing that has brought you face-to-face with your demons - it's not personal. I know it *feels* personal, but that's just because your demons dance well together. Really it's the universe, providing you a personalized lesson in something cosmic. Are you grateful yet?

Your lesson could be made manifest through a lover who won't stop cheating on you, a partner who can't decide to go straight or gay, a parent who abuses you, a kid who's hooked on drugs, a spouse who wants divorce, or your inability to lose weight. Whatever your situation, the particulars are not actually important. They're quirky variations in the way the universe is handing out your particular lesson in fear, and the only way through it is through.

Osho once said that once you go through fear to the other side, there exists nothing but love. Are you willing to go there?

Serena says: I remember taking my husband to the Metro one day, maybe three years into my marriage. I was trying to tackle head-on this issue with him that had been a thorn in my side right from the get-go. It had to do with him always wanting to touch and be with other women. He was stubbornly insisting that I was seeing problems where there weren't any, and I was stubbornly insisting that his behavior was inappropriate, when I suddenly got tired of the sound of my own voice confronting and confronting. I stopped. How many times had we argued variations on this theme, and to no avail? I then thought to myself, "You have a choice, Serena. You can leave this marriage, or you can accept your husband for who he is."

I shrugged and said, "I'm so tired of having this conversation and I'm never going to mention it again." That was it. It wasn't that the problem was solved, but I had stopped trying to solve it. I was done, and a certain peace came over me.

I waited for Greg to get out of the car but he didn't. After a minute he said, "It must be frustrating to ask again and again for the same thing." That was all. He got out, caught his train, and his behavior was different from that day on.

Luckily, there's not a "right way" to handle your life. There's simply the way you're handling it, and that's what there is. When you're looking for help and direction, there is nothing other than what your body says is the right thing to do. This is *inner guidance* and there's no one more adept at guiding you than *you*.

So go. Launch. Find your bliss and follow it. When there's an issue in your life, confront it. Speak your truth about it. Clear your emotions about it. Set your boundaries about it. Do the work, but remember that you're doing the work so that you can enjoy your life. So that you can be open to intimacy. So you can be free, with none of the past issues always dragging you backwards. You'll know you're there when you can embrace everything there is about you, the good, the bad, and the indifferent.

Love, the Catalyst for Change

You have lessons to learn in this life, and one of the greatest ways you'll learn them is by falling in love. A lot will come up. Let it come. Bring it on, baby! When you're in love with someone your energy is amplified in a certain way. Both the dark and the light inside you are more intense. Maybe your journey feels like a lifetime of choosing partners who drive you to misery, but that's just you resisting the lesson until you're ready. I don't mean that harshly. Hey, I'm on this planet too, remember? I have my lessons to learn and partners who have challenged me to the core. No one is exempt, but neither is anyone condemned to a lifetime of loneliness and fear.

When you come up against a big issue, a lifetime-sized issue, you're also going to come up against all your previous methods of coping. By coping, I mean all the things you do to keep in place all the same patterns that were laid down many years ago and are so hard to let go of now. This is why *Full Contact Confrontation* is the eighth law, and not the first. All your old tricks are going to come to the fore, and you'll need all your new tricks to combat them.

Remember you're doing this work to bring bliss into your life as well as mind-blowing intimacy and love, right? You're not doing this to feel worse. You're doing it to feel better, to find more than relief. You're doing it so you can be tender and loving with yourself and thus be able to gift that to others in your life. You may not believe me yet, but strength doesn't come from self-denial and cruelty; strength comes from self-nurturing. This is the reason to follow the Tantric Laws of Intimacy. It's not punishment; it's reward.

So look straight into *The Mirror of Your Beloved* and see yourself. Observe and note the deep patterns that called you to this relationship, and notice what you're doing in the same old way to keep the same old patterns in place. Confront yourself and your partner *deeply*; get to the bottom of these mysteries together. When you can do this without judgment or blame for either one of you, you'll be able to interrupt patterns that have kept you away from intimacy your whole romantic life. You should feel like a hero as well because you've been brave. In the face of fear you've opened up. You've taken on the beasts of a lifetime and that's damn good work!

In *Law VIII: Full Contact Confrontation*, you've learned how to:

- Deal with your demons, drama, destruction and desire.

- Brave the stormy weather of your emotions in sharing your deep inner truths with your partner.

- Appreciate that love is the catalyst not only for bliss, but for deep inner change and transformation.

- Understand that confrontation does not have to lead to destruction.

- Understand and confront your fears about confrontation.

- Understand how the previous eight laws of Tantric Intimacy are a process you need to work through to open yourself to your full potential for love in relation with yourself, and with others.

- Understand that you are confronting your own inner demons in the process of confronting your partner.

- Witness and process the process as you journey through it.

- *Full Contact Confrontation* can open the gateway to bliss.

Once that gateway is open, you have to make the choice to walk through it. *Law IX: Surrender* will guide you on the next part of this journey toward Tantric Intimacy, and the blissful relationship you've always longed for.

Law IX
Surrender

Love has nothing to do with what you are expecting to get—only with what you are expecting to give—which is everything.

– Katherine Hepburn

To circulate energy freely throughout the body and heart requires that we face, embrace, and feel through our fears, moment to moment. Surrender is the texture of no-fear.

– David Deida

Most people don't like the word *Surrender*. There are too many connotations of losing associated with it, of being unwillingly overcome by a more powerful force. "Surrender?" you ask, horrified. "No freaking way! I'll fight to the bitter end!" I know that. But when I speak of *Surrender*, I'm speaking about something altogether different.

The Monkey Trap

Did you ever hear about how monkeys are caught? Bananas are placed in specially designed traps. When a monkey sees the banana, he reaches in to grab it and then finds he can't escape. With his hand in a fist, his hand won't slip back out the bars of the trap. He can't escape the trap because he won't let go of the banana. If he would just let go, he could easily slide his hand out, but he doesn't want to let go of that banana, so there he stays, as trapped as he can be.

Now picture your mind wrapped around a lot of bananas. Each banana represents something you're attached to; in fact, something you cling to, grasp at as essential. Each banana represents an idea that traps you just as the bananas trap those monkeys in a cage. Everyone has closets full of attachments – thoughts, beliefs, things, clothes, expectations about "the way it's supposed to be" with you and your partner.

So the question becomes, how do you convince your monkey mind to let go of its bananas?

My Life is at Stake! Isn't It?

In the case of the monkey, you can easily see that the whole thing is based on survival. It is in you, too. Your reptile brain is trying to keep your identity intact. In other words, it's ego survival. You think, "If I don't have this anymore, I'll die," or "If I let go of control (what control?), I will crash and die." Everybody has this mild irrational fear, right? Right. It's hard-wired into your personality.

Tantra teaches you to think of surrender in a different way. *Surrender* in Tantra means just to let go of your endless battles. *Surrender* is relinquishing the incessant chatter and grasping of your monkey mind to open up your heart and have faith in the larger workings of the world and your right place in it. It is the ultimate *let go*.

The Need to Win

What does surrender mean to you? Think about what you've been fighting for your whole life. Include in that how much you do. Look at the doing-ness of your life as part of the fight, part of the struggle to survive. Now, instead of fantasizing about winning, as if you are a great warrior and everything in life is a contest to the death, imagine instead that you *Surrender*.

Wait, though. I didn't say *lose*, I said *Surrender*. Can you imagine doing that? Go deep into your body and breathe into your awareness. *Be Your Own Witness* for a minute and see if you can find where you store your need to be right and to win.

Nothing Doing

The way humans are made it is as if everything is automatically a fight, even when it is not. Imagine yourself not doing anything for a moment. Can you tell which chakra is activated? Tune in to the tight places in your body and see what's going on. See if you get a headache, or neck pains, or a stomach ache while you're reading this chapter. Just notice for now, that's all.

Okay, let's take this further. Imagine being in the middle of a battle with your partner that is the most exhausting, depressing thing in your life. Imagine that you're trying to be heard, you're struggling to be understood, you're desperate to defend yourself against an unfair attack, to protect yourself from the heartbreaking viciousness of the person you love, but *nothing's working*. The spiraling down has begun. You're descending into that cold and lonely, familiar-feeling place where you were abandoned long ago. Or is that bitter, berserker rage you fear so much erupting right up through your system and wreaking havoc upon your relationship? Maybe you're shutting down, checking out emotionally, whether you physically leave or not. It's all happening, all the behaviors of a lifetime, compressed into this one terrible moment that occurs over and over in your relationship.

Okay, now rest for a moment. Again, tune in to your body and breathe. Imagine that you just stop the whole thing. I don't mean you walk out, I mean just stop. Take a tiny step back, there in your mind, and be an impartial, indifferent witness. Suspend all judgments for a minute and look at yourself. Can you see how afraid you are of losing? Losing what? Breathe and take a good look. Look what's been triggered in you. From out here it's as though you climbed onto a demonically possessed merry-go-round and forgot that the control switch is there in your hands. You can stop! You can stop the whirling torment without even bringing in the notion of winning or losing. But wait, I'm getting ahead of myself.

Letting Go

To demonstrate letting go, let me first give you an example of not letting it go. Rush hour on a Friday afternoon, trying to get out of the city, you can't believe the traffic. No, really, you can't believe it. In fact, you sit there in your car, along with half a million other people all doing the same thing, denying that it could be this way, even though it *is*, right in front of your eyes. You might as well deny the tides as deny being caught in a traffic jam. Intellectually you know this, but you waste huge energy railing against the traffic anyway, resisting what is. Resisting *what is* is a useless and painful exercise, and a hard habit to break.

Surrender means simply embracing *what is* about your life. In the practical sense, surrender means letting go of the idea that you can force the world (or a person) into being what you want. That all your expectations in your monkey mind are naturally going to be met. And if they aren't, you're damned well going to make them get met! And if you can't, then you'll be stuck seething in every traffic jam in your life, or fly off the handle every time someone says no to you, or doesn't celebrate your birthday EXACTLY the way you want.

Learning to surrender these expectations is key in a relationship, because, let's face it, everyone in the world wants to be happy. The key is knowing what makes you happy, and having the courage to express those most intimate inner truths. But they are not carved in stone. They change over time, with different partners. No one is a mind reader, and you change, grow, develop, become curious, want a little variety or spice.

As your monkey mind lets go of its bananas, intimacy has a chance to grow. As you surrender your expectations, you might stop grumbling about all the things you don't have but think you ought to.

Once you stop letting your monkey mind gripe and criticize constantly, you might even find yourself appreciating all the wonderful things you do have. And actually begin considering all sorts of new possibilities in your relationship. That is the beauty of Tantric Intimacy. No matter how long you've been together as a couple, the spirit of the quest helps you fall in love all over again, and helps keep things fresh, new, alive, ecstatic as you move forward in intimacy.

Surrender in the sexual sense means relaxing the grip of your mind over how you think sex "should" be, and how your lover should be making it happen just *that* way. Surrender is letting go of the idea of forcing an outcome. Surrender is letting go of automatic doing. It's giving yourself willingly to the sex-love-life energy of the universe and letting it take you wherever it takes you, trusting that that's the place you need to go, you want to go, you choose to go.

Let Love Open the Door

Take a deep breath, because I want to talk about surrendering to a mind-blowing concept. Can you believe, even briefly, that your beloved would do anything in the world for you if you really needed it, despite the terrible fight you might have had over coffee this morning or about the bills last night? Can you, somewhere in your heart, accept that your partner – the one you say drives you so nuts and makes you so sad – actually wants you to be happy? Actually, whether you have a romantic partner or not, I'm asking if you can believe that you are truly lovable?

Tough one, eh? Here, let me share with you a story of deep intimacy that took place for one of my students while she was receiving oral pleasure from her lover. She was having a battle with herself. As many of you probably know from personal experience, she could have turned the fight outside, onto her partner, but she chose to keep witnessing that the fight was really inside her. As she witnessed, she kept letting go, opening more and more to love. She went deeper and deeper into allowing herself to receive.

Katrina says: "I was in a crazy mood one night, and behaved really badly with my boyfriend. He was upset, and trying to talk reason to me, but I couldn't stop myself. I even left. When I finally exhausted myself ranting and raving and came back to the house, we made love, but it didn't reach me.

The next morning we tried again. This time he laid me out on the bed and very tenderly began going down on me. I knew that he was doing it specially to show me how much he loved me, and that he forgave me. It didn't matter, though; I couldn't relax. He kept going, in no hurry at all, really into it, you know? Still, I almost asked him to stop.

Then I thought, why would I do that? Not because of how it felt. It felt good, but I was self-conscious about taking so long, about not coming, and about being so whacked-out the night before. Just as an experiment, in a way, I stopped myself from stopping him. I let him go on. I thought, "He can stop when he wants to. I'm not going to control everything. I'm going to see where this takes me."

He kept going, trying to tell me with his mouth that everything was okay, only I couldn't believe him. Then it occurred to me that I was actually afraid to believe him. I was afraid to relax and give him this secret part of myself because of how I had been the night before. I was so ashamed!

As he worked on me, though, images began floating through my mind. One was of a solid black stone that felt cold and heavy and seemed to be in the way of me and pleasure. That stone was my shame, blocking me not only from orgasm, but also from sharing myself with my lover. Still he kept going, patient and loving, and also hot for me; I could feel it in his mouth, could feel how much he wanted me. I was so tuned in to my second chakra that I was almost having visions. It felt like if I opened up there, I was going to show him my soul.

And then, between one moment and the next, I decided to. I just gave him everything, opened everything, let him into the deepest, sweetest, most secret part of me, and I knew when I did it that this wasn't just sex and wasn't just an orgasm; it was something transcendent. I was washed so clean. I was forgiven. I was bathed in love that truly felt divine."

Now here's the real question. Was she opening to her love for him or was she opening to self-love? I assert that her body, and this particular act of sex, demonstrated her opening to self-love. Sex was the door. Her partner perhaps sensed her conflict intuitively, and kept loving her through the sex, through her moment-by-moment choice to let go of fear, to push past it. This was the key. The letting go that happened changed her life forever. Maybe it changed his life, too.

In the example above, Katrina is right; it wasn't just sex as usual that morning. It was *Surrender* and *Surrender* and *Surrender* again. The fight was going on inside her, and when she surrendered, rather than lose anything, she won. This is a true example of sacred sex, a true example of the transformative property of Tantra. She actually lost herself (the ego, the separation) and gained the entire universe. Possibly what we are all fighting with is inside us, and we pick partners who bring it out. Then we get an infinite number of chances to surrender again and again, until we finally do. Or do we?

Un-Defending Your Life

Surrender is dropping your defenses. Scary thought, huh? Yeah, surrendering takes real *cojones*. But if you want mind-blowing intimacy and love, well, there's only one way to go. See, you're focused either on loving yourself or on defending yourself. The focus can only be on one or the other. You're breathing the air of love or you're sniffing the fumes of fear. It's your choice. If your partner is not being loving, it's because your partner is focused on being afraid.

The same goes for you. You can break up with a person and do it full of love if you're not letting the fear rule you. Full of love and completely connected, you can ask someone to treat you more respectfully – even while noticing you're afraid. If you are seeing love through the eyes of love, you can honor someone's request without taking it personally. I'm suggesting that you feel and embrace whatever fear, and choose to love anyway.

When you choose to surrender, you choose to stop wasting your precious energy on fear and defensiveness and you begin down the wildly different path of acceptance and trust instead. You choose love. After your childhood programming of fairy tales and Hollywood movies, you might think love just happens, but no. You have to choose to love consciously, over and over again. It seems harder than reacting in fear and hostility because it is. Choosing love requires conscious awareness.

When you use the witness and really look at yourself, you'll see fear lurking under your defensiveness and upset every time. It's true for you and it's true for your darling. If things have gotten ugly, whether for five minutes or for five years, you can bet your bottom dollar the reason is that you became afraid and reptile brain reared its head. In a second of fear you forgot to love and began to war. Here's the really weird thing about this phenomenon: The foundation of all your fear is the fear of losing love. The fear of losing love makes you behave defensive, aggressive, and distant. In short, the fear of losing love makes you act unlovable. What kind of crazy strategy is that?! It makes no sense.

So how do you move from fear to love? You witness the fear, and then you embrace it in yourself rather than resist it or make it wrong. You use all the other laws and you *Surrender*. I will tell you the choice to surrender takes a lot of courage! Are you up for it? I hope so.

The Far, Far Right

I've been talking about giving up the battle, but I haven't named what the battle really is. Do you want to know? It's a very long fight, loudly or quietly, to be the one who's not wrong. Put another way, it's the battle to be right.

Let me tell you how important it is for you to be right. You'd actually lose the love of your life rather than be wrong, and I mean that literally.

You would rather let the love of your life walk out the door forever than admit to being wrong in a fight. It sounds crazy, but you'd rather lose love itself than let go of an *idea* you have about love or how you expect to live your life. It's *that* important to be right. You say love should look like *this*, but your lover says love should look like *that*, and because you disagree and have to be right, you'll just boot love out the door rather than try seeing it from your lover's point of view.

It hardly stops there. Consider that many people would rather do without sex than lose a fight. They opt to shrivel up and dry out the juiciest parts of themselves so they can be "in control" and "right" this time around. I personally know people who have gone for decades at a stretch, years and years of sexless living, rather than back down or say, "I'm so upset and you're so upset, gosh, maybe I should try looking at this differently."

If you're like most people, you feel as though you have to be perfect to be loved, and if you admit to a mistake, I guess, you're no longer perfect. Such a banana!

Down By the Riverside

To *Surrender* is to lay down your sword and shield and admit that all you really want is to love and be loved. I'm talking about *choosing* to surrender to love. It's amazingly freeing. It's choosing to notice and focus on the deep love and respect actually underlying all the resentment and fear in your life.

When you surrender, you consciously let go of your grip on anger and grief long enough to open to love. The love is always there, by the way, but mostly you can't feel it. To feel it, you have to intervene in reptile brain's madness and choose to remember love. Open your fist and let go of the banana.

I should mention that your mind is not going to do this easily. Your mind will kick and scream about it. Your mind is addicted to obsessing over problems, and looks for them everywhere. *Surrender* is the ninth law and the last law discussed in this book because you need to practice at *Being Your Own Witness* and *Releasing Your Emotions*. Then you can walk into your house every day after work and choose to breathe the air of love instead of the strangely habit-forming fumes of fear. Only then will you be able to *Make Love in the Unknown*.

Flip-Flops

Here's something weird about people: We really don't believe in love. I mean as a romantic concept, sure. As something you feel for your pets and kids, yeah, it goes without saying. But love you for who you truly are? Ha! You don't believe you can really be loved. Your secret belief is that you're too disgusting to love.

The flip side of this is that this thinking means you can't love anyone else, either. Flip, flop, flip, flop. Can't love, can't be loved, can't love, and can't be loved. Ah, but then there are the moments of respite. Oh, boy, does the love come flooding in then. Wow, your mind is like a still mountain lake. You love with all the power of your hot spongy heart. Love from someone feels like warm honey pouring over your skin. You surrender to love and find it's the place of no fear. It's heaven on earth in your body – for an instant.

The next morning you get a traffic ticket and you're late to work and your pants are tight and you forgot to pay your credit card bill. Obviously you suck. You're not worthy. You decide to have a talk with your lover to feel better, but when you get off the phone you feel worse. You two aren't on the same wavelength. You shouldn't be together. It'll never work out. He or she thinks you're an idiot and, frankly, you think he or she is an idiot. There's no such thing as love. Maybe there is for other people, but not for you. In short, you're doomed.

Does this monkey mind grasping at these bananas sound all too familiar? So how do you truly let go? How do you get to the place of *Surrender*, of love overflowing, self-love, love for your partner and love for everyone else? How can you get love to last more than a fleeting moment of bliss?

Indifference

Once you have used the tools in the previous chapters for a while, you'll begin to come to a very peaceful place. While being your own witness, you will notice a feeling of indifference. In Zen this is called non-attachment. In this place you'll find less drama and more empowerment.

So I'm coaching you to *be* consciously indifferent, unattached, but not detached. If you cling to your former ideas about the way love should be, this clinging shows itself as the source of your misery. It is the fist clutching the banana. Open your hand/your heart. Let go. Let yourself fall into the unknown. Then just *Be Your Own Witness* throughout your experience. Just watch everything from a place of non-attachment, of not trying to force outcomes, while choosing love. Whatever there is coming at you in life – accept it. Then choose to bring your energies more and more towards trust and love. Look, you can use your energy any which way you choose. You can use it to doubt your feelings or your partner's feelings, as you have been in all of your previous relationships, or you can use the same energy to trust. The moment you let go of your expectations, and are indifferent to the outcome, recognizing that in fact there doesn't have to be any outcome except love and bliss, you'll see that you can work with your energy from an empowered state.

Then once again bring your attention to love. Love more. That leads to more love. Then love even more. This leads to even more love. You live in a more loving way not just towards yourself, but towards your partner, and towards everything that exists. Inside the place of non-attachment, nothing is right, nothing is wrong. Simply choose love.

At the ninth law of Tantric Intimacy, *Surrender*, you empty yourself of attachment to feelings, attachment to having to be right. You empty yourself of anger, of fear. When you are empty, your former self somehow disappears. You are and you are not. One thing for sure is that you are not the same you that you've always known. This is a good thing. The real *you* becomes the one that is conscious. With this new-found awareness, you can dissolve the entire past.

In my life, this has been a shocking revelation. All of a sudden when I witness how whole I have become, I see that I no longer even need the boundaries I set. I know, I know. I said earlier that *Setting Your Boundaries* was important in intimacy. At an earlier point it is. As you follow these principles, suddenly you too will become whole and empty at the same time, even though it seems like a contradiction. You may feel that I am being contradictory by even telling you this. I promise, when you empty yourself out and you are good and empty, you can expect to lose the need for boundaries.

Now there can be a meeting, a merger with another person, with your partner, to a level of intimacy never before attained because there is the space for it. There, in the emptiness, you are whole and you need nothing from the other person.

Mind you, reptile brain is in there all the time trying to protect itself, while monkey mind will still get up to mischief, and try to hold on to all the bananas. It definitely doesn't want you to let go to this place I am talking about, but take a look. It has to be better than where you have been or even are right now, or you wouldn't be reading this book.

Picture this: You and your lover are sitting side by side. If you both have consciously let go of attachment to being right (to your egos) or attachment to doing, then what is possible for you is the ultimate in intimacy. To say mind blowing is almost too little or clichéd a word. The deep inner sexual energy we talked about at the start of this book can move anywhere between you, and around you, and through you.

Through this energy and intimacy, you can lose yourself and experience supreme orgasm. You can lose all identity, and you can fall into the abyss of the unknown. This, my friends, is Tantra.

Now usually when this happens, if you have stumbled onto it, it happens for only a moment because we begin to cling or get attached to this incredibly blissful moment. We let fear come in, and we become afraid of losing the partner, or losing ourselves to the partner. Maybe we become afraid of dying, or fear that the molecules will become too loose or that we will go berserk. Or we start to fear we may never experience such joy and bliss again.

With Tantra, people are able to experience this supreme orgasm for longer and longer periods of time because it involves relaxing into love, rather than love "making," relaxing into surrender - allowing rather than doing. There is no making or doing in this place of profound bliss. All connection happens without effort.

In this place there is nothing to resist, nothing more needed, nothing more to be had or achieved, no performance, nothing that should or shouldn't be present. So if anger shows up, no problem. You have been doing all the Tantric hard work: *Emotional Release, Setting Boundaries, Speaking Your Truth.* You have been following these principles. Now when you let go of anticipation or expectations, whatever shows up simply shows up. There is no need to attach to it. If you leave it alone, and witness it with indifference, but do not attach to it, it will come and go as gently as the wind blows. No big effort is necessary now. This is the conscious act of choosing love.

If you're wondering how long all this is going to take you, my answer is not long. I have discovered that it is simply not a terribly long process although when you are first starting out, it seems like such deep doodoo, with you in the mess so far you think you'll never get out. At first, you may feel totally alone, but this is only a passing phase. Don't attach to that either. If you can simply focus on receiving, you will have it.

You might try sex with your partner in this fashion. One night you can decide simply to give to your partner for hours. Give and give, while your partner surrenders simply to receiving. The next night you can surrender to receiving while your partner gives to you for hours. On the third night, go back to having sex in a more conventional way. See how it is, just witness each in turn and keep your monkey mind open to the ideas and possibilities each night brings.

When you finally surrender completely, you open to the deepest valley of receptivity. Then the highest peaks of consciousness can be given to you. You begin to see the gift, the Divine in yourself and in your Beloved. You have opened to the cosmic consciousness.

In Tantric Intimacy *Law IX: Surrender*, you've learned:

- To let go of the need to win, to be right.

- That the expectations about love you grasp so tightly actually drive love out of your life.

- That expectations of a person or relationship stop love from growing and relationships from thriving.

- That non-attachment to outcomes is the way to a blissful inner peace.

- That non-attachment allows you to be open to all possibilities in your life, especially with your lover.

- That you can only let love in if you throw fear out.

- That intimacy is all about trust; trust yourself, trust your partner, trust the process.

- In this spirit of new-found trust, be willing to experiment in your relationship with an open mind and heart, and then just witness what happens, without judging.

Now you can go back to the chapter I started this book with. Once you allow yourself to *Surrender*, you are ready to take that step. You can surely *Make Love in the Unknown.* I took you all this way through the other nine laws of Tantric Intimacy in order to get you back to the delectable dessert, the place where we started, the Tantric concept of sex according to me. Re-read the tenth law, and then open your arms and get ready for mind-blowing intimacy. You've earned it!

XI

What to do now?

Love is, above all else, the gift of oneself.

– Jean Anouilh

So now you've re-read Tantric Intimacy Law X: *Make Love in the Unknown*, what now? What do you do? Where do you start? What can you do next? To continue with what you've learned. Where can you learn more?

I certainly hope you enjoyed reading this book, but more importantly, I hope you will use these Tantric Laws of Intimacy to dramatically enhance your life. In my experience, reading alone will not make the difference you are looking for. Reading is a start, but if you want to succeed, it's your actions that are going to make the difference.

Throughout this book, I introduced many concepts that may have been foreign to you. Perhaps some were familiar, but others were radically different, like *making love in the unknown*, practicing *emotional release*, or even *speaking your truth*. Please make sure you do these practices regularly so that you can begin to redefine your relationship with intimacy and eventually to shift your habitual behavior patterns with your partner or your partner to be.

In order to alter your relationship with intimacy permanently, the change must occur on a cellular level. Your brain's wiring must be re-patterned. For this to occur, you must put the material we have discussed into practice for yourself. Luckily, it does not take long.

I recommend that you commit to the practices offered here and that you re-read the book a few times until you have become familiar enough with the material to form new habits of thinking. New habits of thinking lead to new habits of action. The more you put these principles into action, the faster the concepts will become natural and automatic to you.

You may not think this process easy, but I promise you won't be alone. Remember Laws IX and X, *Surrender*, and *Make Love in the*

Unknown. Instead of clinging to fear, trust to love. Trust your partner. Share this book and these activities with your beloved. To make love, you have to make love.

In addition, I have set up a website to support this book, with worksheets and suggestions for additional activities. Please visit the site at www.lauriehandlers.com.

Namaste

Testimonials

"The experience from the Tantra & Bliss class and the freedom I take with me is amazing...I am so pleased! Thank you again."

– Charlie Reaves, *Mortgage Lending Account Executive*
Winston Salem, NC

"Attending your Tantra & Bliss Intensive was very useful. Afterwards, I felt surer of myself... I have been using the breath a lot more...with success. You teach in a very simple direct fashion holding high expectations for your students. Thank you."

– Marilyn Ladner, *Personal Coach, New York, NY*

"I feel Beautiful! Powerful! Confident! And Extremely Sexual! I am amazed how I feel now compared to before!"

– Carlos, *Promoter/Musician, Toronto, Canada*

"I got to see how much I am loved and appreciated. Part of my work with you and my experience with Tantra & Bliss has been being able to let that love in."

– Colette Mullenmaster, *Graphic Design Artist, Washington, DC*

"Due in large part to Laurie, Butterfly Workshops, Inc. and the wonderful teachings and shift in me being from the Tantra & Bliss Intensive, the Ecstasy Intensive, Leadership, Integrity & Service, the Initiation Spa Retreat course and the Butterfly Tantra weekly groups, I now have the best relationship with a woman I've ever had. My energy was activated by Butterfly Workshops and the enduring manifestation is LOVE."

– Anonymous